D0966027

The Perpetual
ALMANACK
of Folklore

Future

The Perpetual
ALMANACK
of
FOLKLORE

by *CHARLES KIGHTLY*

with 237 illustrations

THAMES AND HUDSON

*To the York Waits
and Punkes' Delight*

© 1987 Thames and Hudson Ltd, London

Printed and bound in Hong Kong

FOREWORD

'To every thing, there is a season, and a time to every purpose under
the Heaven'

Ecclesiastes III.i

'Who is there, that maketh not great account of his almanack to
observe both days, times and seasons, to follow his affairs for his best
profit and use?'

The Christian Almanacke 1612

AN ALMANACK was literally indispensable to the people of Elizabethan, Stuart
and early Georgian Britain. It first of all provided them with a calendar,
showing not only the dates of saints' days and other festivals but also the
waxing and waning of the moon and the seasonal rotation of the heavenly
bodies through the successive astrological houses. These were matters of
great moment, since a sensible farmer would no more think of picking apples
before St Swithin's Day than he would plant corn or slaughter beasts when
the moon was declining, lest the crops and the meat shrank with her: nor
would he cut his weeds (or his hair) when she was waxing, and when they
would grow again with renewed vigour. Neither would anyone in their
right mind marry or begin an important enterprise when the stars in their
courses were set against them, or on any of the traditionally unlucky days laid
down by their almanack. Anything started on the notoriously ill-omened
twenty-eighth of December, for example, was bound to fail disastrously, and
the very day of the week on which that dismal commemoration of the
Massacre of the Innocents fell was to be treated with caution throughout the
succeeding year: while any misguided invalid who embarked on a 'course of
physick' during the star-crossed 'dog days' of July and August was virtually
committing suicide.

FOREWORD

Apart from reminding its users of the duties and dangers of the changing seasons, the almanack also predicted (with an inaccuracy directly proportional to its attempted precision) the weather they could expect at given times, or even on specific days. It likewise furnished them with traditional hints and rhymes for 'prognosticating' the weather for themselves, for instance by noting the thickness of Martinmas ice, the behaviour of cats or hedgehogs, or the appearance of the Michaelmas goose's breastbone. Some almanacks also taught their readers the rudiments of fortune telling and folk physiognomy, thus allowing them to foretell the future of their babies or gauge a stranger's character by the shape of his ears; and a few retailed magical formulae for deciding such vital questions as the identity of a future spouse, whether a girl had lost her virginity, and the whereabouts of the local witch's house.

For the less gullible, such arcane lore was usually interspersed with practical tips on gardening, agriculture and animal husbandry, advice on preserving health (together with hair-raising if not lethal 'remedies'), and culinary 'receipts' suited to the seasonal availability of natural foods. Educational items on the uses of herbs and the surprising habits of birds and beasts were also featured, as were improving moral tales and sensational revelations of monstrous births, narrow escapes, and divine judgments on evil-doers. Almanacks, in short, catered for a very wide range of tastes and needs, and accordingly enjoyed overwhelming popularity: during the seventeenth century alone over two thousand different almanacks were published, and in the 1660s and 70s their collective sales, totalling several hundred thousand a year, easily outstripped those of the Bible.

These entertaining and useful publications, therefore, afford a particularly illuminating insight into the beliefs, modes of thought and lifestyle of our ancestors, and this present Perpetual Almanack strives to reproduce something of their atmosphere for modern readers. It draws its material not only from almanacks and related manuals of prognostication and astrology, but also from a wide range of other relevant popular literature of the Tudor, Stuart and Georgian eras, much of it currently available only in specialist libraries. This includes farming and medical handbooks; herbals both well-known and obscure; printed cookery books and manuscript housekeeping instructions; the works of John Aubrey and other pioneer folklorists; and such ephemera as chapbooks, broadsides and early newspapers.

Like its models, this Perpetual Almanack is also intended to be of practical value to its users, though the exact truth of some of its assertions cannot always be vouched for, and it is perhaps unwise to put too much trust in its advice on prognosticating the weather or the future. The twelve or thirteen days discrepancy between the Old and New Style calendars (see over) should likewise be borne in mind when considering its prophecies and counsels, and traditional practices recommended for (say) May Day could well prove more efficacious if performed on May the thirteenth or fourteenth rather than May the first. Being a Perpetual Almanack for use in any year, moreover, it cannot allow for the annual fluctuations of Easter and other 'movable feasts', instead providing information about them at some convenient date about the mid-point of their range. Finally, while many of the kitchen receipts and milder herbal cures are certainly worth trying out, some of the other remedies may prove a little drastic for modern tastes, and are thus rather to be wondered at than essayed. All this said, the author hopes that this book will render its conscientious users at least as well protected against the changes and chances of the year as were their seventeenth-century ancestors, and as well advised: and since no true almanack ever failed to sing its own praises, he will end with an encomium borrowed from Richard Allestree's almanack of 1622.

Wit, learning, order, elegance of phrase
Health, and the art to lengthen out our days
Philosophy, physic and poesie
All this, and more, is in this book to see

OLD STYLE AND NEW STYLE

THIS ALMANACK contains many references to 'Old Style' and 'New Style', and most major festivals appear twice, for example as 'Midsummer' and 'Old Midsummer Day', respectively June the twenty-fourth and July the fifth. This is because, during the period when most of its sources were written, and when the beliefs and practices they describe grew up, Britain observed a different calendar from that used today, namely the 'Old Style' or 'Julian' calendar. Introduced by Julius Caesar in 45 BC, the old calendar was based on a calculation of the solar year at $365\frac{1}{4}$ days, the extra days being made up by four-yearly 'leap year' days kept on February the twenty-ninth. But the calculation was a slight overestimate, and by the sixteenth century European astronomers had established that a considerable discrepancy had developed between the Julian calendar and the true solar year. In 1582, therefore, Pope Gregory XIII introduced a 'New Style' or 'Gregorian' calendar, correcting the error by missing out ten days.

Though much of Catholic Europe soon afterwards followed suit, staunchly Protestant Britain (and her American Colonies) obstinately held out against the reformed or 'Popish' calendar for another 170 years, and it was not until 1752 (by which time the discrepancy had increased to eleven days) that she finally fell into line with Europe: effecting the change – to the outrage of many Britons – by missing out the days between September the second and September the fourteenth in that year. Most almanacks, therefore, were compiled under the old system, and their advice and weather prognostications remain better suited to it. It is far more likely to snow, for instance, on Old Christmas Day (January the sixth) than on December the twenty-fifth, and though you may often search in vain for blossom on May the first 'New Style', it has nearly always appeared by May the thirteenth – which is usually called Old May Day, though the discrepancy between the old calendar and the solar year has now in fact increased to thirteen days. The whole traditional or customary year has thus 'moved forwards' by nearly two weeks, a fact which readers should take into account.

JANUARY

THE MIDWINTER MONTH

Named after the double-faced Roman God Janus, who looks back
towards the Old and forward to the New Year.

In Welsh: *Ionawr*

In Gaelic: *An ceud Mhìos na Bliadhna* – the first month of the year.

In Anglo-Saxon: *Giuli* – the month of Yule.

JANUARY

New Year's Day: the Seventh Day of Christmas: everything you do today will influence your luck in the coming year.

1

> Love and joy come to you
> And to our wassail too
> And God send you a Happy New Year
>   The Yorkshire Wassail

Nothing should be taken out of the house today – not even rubbish – and especially do not lend fuel or matches, or pay bills, lest you lack fire and money during the coming year. If it is absolutely necessary to carry something out, be sure to bring something in first – preferably a coin, concealed outside on the previous night.

> Take out, then take in
> Bad luck will begin
> Take in, then take out
> Good luck comes about.

Give New Year's gifts (or 'Hogmanays') to your friends and neighbours. A lucky present is an apple stuck with cloves and rosemary or holly, and in Wales the 'Calennig' (New Year) apple should be studded with wheat, oats, nuts and evergreens, floured and gilded, and provided with a tripod stand of holly or rowan skewers. The usual Scots 'Hogmanay' is a fine three-cornered oatcake or shortbread, with 'Yule-kebbuck' or Christmas cheese.

The Eighth Day of Christmas: guard your health, and allay disorders caused by New Year celebrations.

2

> Fly Physic, Sloth, and Venery
> Avoid all Baths most carefully
>   Neve's *Almanack* 1633

'Many there are whom the head whirleth so sore, that he thinketh the earth turneth upside down: the same also hath pain in the eye, and he weeneth that a sort of flies do fly before his eyen. Those may be healed in this wise: they may drink no strong drinks nor wine, without it be very well allayed with much water.'
                    John Hollybush *The Homish Apothecary* 1561

3

The Ninth Day of Christmas: observe the weather, which should be seasonably cold now, since a mild January must be paid for later.

> A kindly good Janiveer
> Freezeth the pot by the fire
>
> If in January, the sun much appear
> March and April pay full dear.

The beautiful but poisonous Christmas Rose, alias Black Hellebore or Bearsfoot, generally flowers about now: and some common Chickweed is usually in flower, or at least green.

'The juice or distilled water of chickweed is of much good use for all heat and redness of the eyes, if some be dropped into them, as also into the ears to ease the pain of them. Little birds in cages (especially linnets) are refreshed with it, when they loath their meat.'

William Coles *Adam in Eden* 1657

4

The Tenth Day of Christmas: make your cake for Twelfth Night.

'To make a Twelfth Cake. Put two pounds of butter in a warm pan and work it to a cream with your hand: then put in two pounds of loaf sugar sifted; a large nutmeg grated; and of cinnamon ground, allspice ground, ginger, mace and coriander each a quarter ounce. Now break in eighteen eggs by one and one, meantime beating it for twenty minutes or above; stir in a gill of brandy: then add two pounds of sifted flour, and work it a little. Next put in currants four pounds, chopped almonds half a pound; citron the like; and orange and lemon peel cut small half a pound. Put in one bean and one pea in separate places, bake it in a slow oven for four hours, and ice it or decorate it as you will.'

Elizabeth Raffald *The Experienced English Housekeeper* 1769

The Eleventh Day of Christmas: Christmas Eve, Old Style.

5

The famous Christmas-flowering Holy Thorns at Glastonbury and elsewhere obstinately adhere to the old dispensation, and are more likely to bloom now than on December the 24th. In 1753, the year after the official calendar change: 'A vast concourse of people attended the noted Thorns on Christmas Eve, New Style: but to their great disappointment, there was no appearance of its blowing: which made them watch it narrowly the 5th of January (or Old Christmas) when it blowed as usual.'

The Gentleman's Magazine 1753

The Twelfth Day of Christmas: Christmas Day, Old Style: the Feast of the Epiphany.

6

> Now Christmas is past; Twelfth Day is the last
> To the Old Year adieu; Great joy to the New
>   Welsh Twelfth Night carol

This was once the most festive day of the Twelve, its celebrations ruled by the King of the Bean and the Queen of the Pea – respectively the man and the woman who found the concealed bean and pea in their slice of Twelfth Cake. If a woman chanced on the bean, however, she could choose the King; while a man who got the 'pea slice' could select the Queen.

The Feast of the Three Kings, or of the Epiphany – a Greek word meaning 'manifestation' – so called because the infant Christ was today revealed to the Three Kings or 'Magi'.

In most parts of the country it is customary to take down Christmas decorations today, and extremely unlucky to leave them up a day longer: in a few places they may remain up until Candlemas in February. Evergreen decorations must never be carelessly discarded: some say they should be ceremonially burnt, while others allow them to rot quietly in the garden.

7

'Saint Distaff's Day': in southern England, the day to begin work again after the Christmas holiday.

> Partly work and partly play
> Ye must on Saint Distaff's day
> From the plough soon free the team
> Then come home and fodder them
> If the Maids a-spinning go
> Burn the flax and fire the tow
> Bring in pails of water then
> Let the Maids bewash the men
> Give Saint Distaff all the right
> Then bid Christmas sport goodnight
> And next morrow, every one
> To his own vocation.

Herrick *Hesperides* 1648

'Saint Distaff' is a jocular canonization of the distaff or 'rock' used by women to hold their unspun wool.

8

Cherish farm animals in bad weather, especially lambing ewes: listen for thunder.

> From every tree the superfluous boughs
> Now prune for thy cattle thereon to go browse
> If snow do continue, sheep hardly that fare
> Crave Mistle and Ivy for them for to spare.
>
> By brambles and bushes, in pasture too full
> Poor sheep be in danger, and looseth their wool
> Now therefore thy ewe, upon lambing so near
> Desireth in pasture that all may be clear.

Tusser *Five Hundred Points of Good Husbandry* 1573

'When in the Time of Winter the Sun is in Capricornus or Aquarius, and especially from Christmas until the Tenth of January, if the Thunder be heard then, then it shall be throughout the whole Year, more windy than any other Year is.'

The Husbandman's Practice 1729

In frosty weather, look to your stored fruit: make apple tarts.

9

'If the frost be very extreme, and you fear the endangering of your fruit, it is good to cover them somewhat thick with fine hay, or else to lay them covered all over either in barley chaff or dry salt: as for laying them in chests of juniper or cypress, it is but a toy, and not worth the practice. If you hang apples in nets within the air of the fire, it will keep them long, but they will be dry and withered, and lose their best relish.'

Markham *The English Husbandman* 1635

'To make Apple-tart. Take apples and peel them, and slice them thin from the core into a pan with white wine, good store of sugar, cinnamon and rose-water, and so boil all till it be thick. Then cool it and strain it, and beat it very well together with a spoon, and then put it into your coffin or crust and bake it. It carrieth the colour red.'

Markham *The English Housewife* 1683

Plough Monday – the first Monday after Twelfth Day – falls about now.

10

Plough Monday, next after that Twelfth Day be past.
Bids out with the plough: the worst husband is last.

In northern and eastern England, this was the day on which ploughing and general farm work was supposed to resume after the Christmas holidays. It was, however, generally given over to a 'Fool Plough' procession of young labourers, variously called Plough Boys, Stots (or Bullocks), Plough Jags or Plough Witches.

In Yorkshire, Northumberland and Durham the decorated Fool Plough was accompanied by a team of sword dancers, who performed a Mumming Play centring upon the mock execution and revival of a 'victim' during an intricate linked-sword dance.

Just now I'm going to die
As you can plainly see
These six fine glittering swords
Will soon put an end to me
Bellerby Sword Dance Play, North Yorkshire

11

New Year's Eve or Hogmanay, Old Style: witches active again after Christmas.

'Henry Hatfield of Rhodes sayeth that Katherine Earle struck him on the neck with a docken stalk, and his mare upon the neck also, whereupon his mare suddenly fell sick and died, and he himself was sore troubled. And the said Katherine hath been searched, and a mark found upon her in the likeness of a pap. And the said Katherine clapped one Mr Frank between the shoulders with her hand, and said, "You are a pretty gentleman; will you kiss me?": whereupon the said Mr Frank fell sick before he got home, and never went out of door after, but died.'

York Castle Trial Records, January the 11th 1655

'A charm to find who hath bewitched your cattle. Put a pair of breeches upon the cow's head, and beat her out of the pasture with a good cudgel upon a Friday, and she will run right to the witch's door and strike thereat with her horns.'

Reginald Scot *The Discovery of Witchcraft* 1584

12

The yellow-flowered groundsel – whose name means 'ground-swallower', because it covers any unused land so quickly – continues to bloom even at this bleak season: and so does shepherd's purse, so called because its heart-shaped seed-pods resemble a medieval pouch.

'This herb groundsel is Venus's mistress-piece, and is as gallant and universal a medicine for all diseases coming of heat, in what part of the body they be, as the sun shines upon.'

Culpeper *Herbal* 1653

'Shepherd's purse stayeth bleeding in any part of the body, whether the juice or decoction thereof be drunk, or whether it be used poultice-wise, or in bath, or any way whatever.'

Gerard *Herbal* 1633

St Hilary's Day, traditionally the coldest day of the year: marriages once again permitted after the Advent and Christmas ban.

13

'The form of the wedding ring being circular, that is round and without end, imparteth thus much, that their mutual love and affection should roundly flow from one to the other as in a circle, and that continually and forever.'

Henry Swinburne *Treatise of Spousals* 1686

The wedding ring is worn on the third finger of the left hand, because it was believed that 'from thence ran a Particular Vein straight to the Seat of Love, the Heart'. It must never be worn before the ceremony, but thereafter should never be removed for long, and certainly never lent to anyone.

> As your wedding ring wears
> So your cares wear away.

Very cold weather usual at this season.

14

'The old Lord Grey, when he was Deputy of Ireland, to inure his sons for the Wars, would usually in the depth of Winter, in frost, snow, rain and what weather soever befell, cause them at midnight to be raised out of their beds, and carried abroad a-hunting till the next morning: then perhaps come wet and cold home, having for breakfast a brown loaf and a mouldy cheese or (which is three times worse) a dish of Irish butter. And on this manner the Spartans and Laconicans dieted and brought up their childen.'

Henry Peacham *The Compleat Gentleman* 1634

15

Take good care of hounds in hard weather: beware ice skating.

'Now for the ordering of your Hounds after they have done hunting, you shall as soon as you bring them into the Kennel, wash all their feet either with a little warm butter and beer, with beef broth, or water wherein mallows and nettles have been boiled soft and tender; and search the foot for thorns, stubs, or any other pricklings. . . . If it be in the strength of Winter, after they are fed you shall suffer them for an hour or two to beak and stretch themselves before the fire . . . but that once finished, you shall force them from the fire, and make them find out their Lodgings.'

Markham *Country Contentments* 1615

'It is estimated, that no less than a dozen persons have lost their lives in this last week, by unadvisedly skating upon thin ice, which broke and drowned them: whereof five expired at one time, within the sight of some fifty spectators in St James's Park.'

York Courant 15th of January 1748

16

Greet the first new moon of the New Year, when it appears.

'At the first appearance of the New Moon after New Year's Day, go out in the Evening and stand astride the Bars of a Gate, or Stile (In Yorkshire they kneel on a ground-fast Stone) looking on the Moon, and say:

All Hail to the Moon, all Hail to thee
I prithee good Moon reveal to me
This Night who my Husband (or Wife) must be.

You must presently after go to Bed. I knew two Gentlewomen that did thus when they were young Maids, and they had Dreams of those that afterwards Married them.'

John Aubrey *Miscellanies* 1695

Twelfth Night, Old Style: wassail your apple trees.

17

This is the proper time for 'wassailing' apple trees, to encourage them to bear a good crop in the coming year. In the apple-growing areas of southern and western England, festive parties assembled in orchards by night to sing to the trees, drink their health, and pour buckets of hot cider over their roots: cider-soaked toast was then left in the branches for the guardian birds, and finally a great 'howl' was raised, while guns were fired into the air to frighten away evil spirits.

Old apple tree, we wassail thee, and hoping thou wilt
bear
For the Lord doth know, where we shall be, till apples
come another year
To bear well and bloom well, so merry let us be
Let every man take off his hat and shout to the old
apple tree.
Old apple tree, we wassail thee, and hoping thou wilt
bear
Hats full, caps full, three-bushel bags full
And a little heap under the stairs.

Apple Tree Wassail, North Somerset

Old Twelfth Day: lambing well under way in most lowland areas.

18

'If a lamb be born sick and weak, the Shepherd shall fold it in his cloak, blow into the mouth of it, and then drawing the Dam's dug, shall squirt milk into the mouth of it. If an Ewe grow unnatural, and will not take her Lamb after she hath yeaned it, you shall take a little of the Clean of the Ewe (which is the bed in which the Lamb lay) and force the Ewe to eat it, or at least chew it in her mouth, and she will fall to love her Lamb naturally. But if an Ewe have cast her Lamb, and you would have her take to another Ewe's Lamb, you shall take the Lamb which is dead, and with it rub and daub the live Lamb all over, and so put it to the Ewe: and she will take to it as naturally as if it were her own.'

Markham *Cheap and Good Husbandry* 1613

19

Days now growing noticeably longer.

> As the days lengthen
> So the cold strengthens.

'To make an excellent Hot Posset. Take half a pint of Sherry-Sack, and as much Rhenish white wine, and sweeten them to your taste with Sugar. Beat ten yolks of Eggs and eight whites, sweeten these also, and pour them to the wine, adding a stick or two of Cinnamon bruised: and set this dish to heat strongly but not to boil; yet it must begin to thicken. In the meantime boil for a quarter of an hour three pints of Cream seasoned with Sugar and some Cinnamon. Then take it from boiling, but let it continue scalding hot while the wine is heating. When both are as hot as they can be without boiling, pour the Cream into the wine from as high as you can. When all is in, set it to stew for one eighth of an hour, then sprinkle all about the top the juice of a quarter of a Lemon, and if you will you may strew on Powder of Cinnamon and Sugar.'

The Closet of Sir Kenelm Digby Opened 1669

20

The Eve of St Agnes' Day: a time for lovers' divinations.

The historical St Agnes was a thirteen-year-old Christian maiden, who chose martyrdom rather than marriage to a pagan Roman officer: she is therefore the patroness of young girls and of bodily chastity, but is nevertheless popular with lovers.

To be sure to dream of your future husband tonight, fast strictly and keep silent all day, and on no account allow anyone – even a child – to kiss you. At bedtime, donning the best and cleanest nightdress you have, boil an egg hard: take out the yolk, fill the space with salt, and eat the egg, shell and all. Then walk backwards to bed, saying:

> Fair St Agnes, play thy part
> And send to me my own sweetheart
> Not in his best or worst array
> But in the clothes he wears every day.

You will then see your intended in your sleep: but tell nobody of your dream.

St Agnes' Day: the Sun enters the House of Aquarius.

21

'The man born under Aquarius shall be lonely and ireful; he shall have silver at thirty-two years; he shall win wherever he goeth, or he shall be sore sick. He shall have fear on the water and afterwards have good fortune, and shall go into divers strange countries. He shall live to be seventy-five years after nature.

'The woman shall be delicious, and have many noises for her children; she shall be in great peril at twenty-four years, and thereafter in felicity. She shall have damage by beasts with four feet: and shall live seventy-seven years after nature.'

The Kalendar of Shepheardes 1604

St Vincent's Day: observe the weather – and the legs, which are ruled by Aquarius.

22

Remember on St Vincent's Day
If that the Sun his beams display
For 'tis a token, bright and clear
Of prosperous weather all the year.

'The legs slender, signifieth one to be dull of capacity (yet this faileth often in Learned Students); the calves very big, bearing out, to be sluggish and rude mannered; the calves meanly big formed, to be witty and honest conditioned. The legs big-sinewed and brawned, to be strong; small-sinewed, to be libidinous; big and ill-fashioned, to be unshamefaced; the parts about the ankles over-fleshy, to be foolish.'

The Shepherd's Prognostication 1729

23

Plant quickset hedges.

'The Whitethorn is esteemed the best for hedges: it is raised either of seeds or plants, but by plants is the speediest way. Let your plants be about the bigness of your thumb, if you can, and set almost perpendicular. The plants being young should be carefully fenced with a dry hedge, from the biting of cattle on both sides, until the tops are quite out of their reach: and it is a piece of good husbandry to plant setters at some convenient intervals, either of timber trees proper to the soil, or of crab-apples and pear-stocks, which will very much improve the land for the future and commend the industry of the planter.'

Worlidge *Systema Agriculturae* 1697

24

Keep good watchdogs about you, these dark nights.

'The watch-dog ought to be horrible, fierce, strange and unacquainted with all except his master, so that he be always at daggers-drawing, and ready to fight with all which shall but lay hands on him. For which cause he ought to be instructed from his littering: let him often be provoked by boys; and as he groweth, let some stranger set on him with weapon, with whom let him combat, and then let him tear some piece of the provoker's garment, that so he may depart with the conceit of victory. These dogs ought to be black-coloured, and great mouthed for barking bigly, so that he may terrify the thief both night and day.'

Edward Topsell *The History of Four-footed Beasts* 1607

'To know whether a sick man shall live or die. Take a little of their water and put it into milk. If they will die, a dog will not drink the milk; or if they will live, a dog will lap it greedily.'

Fairfax Household Book, 17th/18th century

The Feast of the Conversion of St Paul: Burns Night.

25

If the day of St Paul prove clear
Then shall betide a happy year
If it chance to snow or rain
Then shall be dear all kinds of grain
But if high winds shall be aloft
Wars shall vex this realm full oft
And if thick mists make dark the sky
Both beasts and fowls this year shall die.

Erra Pater 1694

On this day in 1759 Robert Burns was born, and Scots everywhere celebrate their national poet's birthday with Burns Suppers, whose centrepiece is the famous haggis:

Fair fa' your honest sonsie face
Great chieftain o' the pudden race
Abune them a' ye tak your place
Painch, tripe, or thairm
Weel are ye worthy o' a grace
As lang's my airm

Burns *Address to a Haggis*

Shun winter melancholy at this dark season.

26

'To bedward be you merry, or have merry company about you, so that to bedward no anger nor heaviness, sorrow or pensiveness, do trouble or disquiet you. To bedward, and also in the morning, use to have a fire in your chamber, to waste and consume the evil vapours, for the breath of man may putrefy the air within the chamber. When you be in your bed, lie a little while on your left side, and sleep on your right side. Let your nightcap be of scarlet, and in your bed lie not too hot or too cold, but in a temperance.'

Andrew Boorde *The Dietary of Health* 1547

'He that is become mad with sadness and heaviness, to him ought fair to be spoken and made merry: many things should be promised him, and some given. If it is a man, let him be refreshed with women, for the same avoideth anger: but if it be a woman, let her be refreshed with men; the same bringeth them soon to their senses.'

John Hollybush *The Homish Apothecary* 1561

27

Do not sleep overlong.

'On this day in 1698 Samuel Clinton, a labouring man of Timbury near Bath, awoke in good health from having slept continually since November the 19th 1697 – on which day he had awoken briefly to ask for bread and cheese, but had fallen asleep again before he could eat it. Previous to that date, he had slept solidly since August the 17th: and before that . . . from April the 9th until August the 7th 1697. . . . All efforts to arouse him (even by injecting smelling salts up his nostrils, or running a great pin into his arm to the bone) had proved in vain.'

Philosophical Transactions 1708

28

Shoot wildfowl, now coming to the end of their season: employing a stalking horse if necessary.

'If the fowl are so shy, and the place so free from shelter, that there be no way to come at them fairly, then you must lead forth your Stalking Horse, being some old Jade trained up for that purpose, and that will not startle much at the report of a Gun. Behind whose shoulders you must shelter yourself: and take your aim before his shoulders, and under his neck, which is better than under his belly. If you have not such a Beast ready, you may make an Artificial one of any old canvas, in shape like a horse feeding on the ground. Let it be made on a sharp stick, that you may fix it in the ground as you have occasion: it must be high enough to conceal your body from the fowl. You may also make an Artificial Ox or Cow, which you may use when your Horse is discovered through much use.'

Worlidge *Systema Agriculturae* 1697

Be careful when you cut your finger nails: listen for the Mistle Thrush.

29

Cut nails on a Monday, cut them for health
Cut them on a Tuesday, cut them for wealth
Cut them on Wednesday, cut them for news
Cut them on Thursday, a pair of new shoes
Cut them on Friday, cut them for sorrow
Cut them on Saturday, see your true love tomorrow
But cut them on Sunday, your safety seek
For Old Nick'll have you, the rest of the week.

White specks on the nail presage good fortune, blue specks ill-luck. White specks on the thumb-nail foreshow honours to come, specks on the fore-finger nail foretell riches.

The Mistle or Mistletoe Thrush, also called Holly Cock, Stormcock or Jeremy (January) Joy, sings loudly at this season, even or especially in rough and tempestuous weather – which her song is said to presage.

On this day in 1649, King Charles I was executed at Whitehall.

30

> He nothing common did or mean
> Upon that memorable scene
> But with his keener Eye
> The Axe's edge did try.
> Andrew Marvell *An Horatian Ode*
> *upon Cromwell's Return* 1650

'Charles Stuart, the now King of England . . . hath had a wicked design totally to subvert the ancient and fundamental laws and liberties of this nation, and in their place to introduce an arbitrary and tyrannical government.'

The Ordinance for the King's Trial

'There was such a consternation among the common people throughout the nation, that one neighbour durst scarcely speak to another when they met in the street – not from an abhorrence of the event, but in surprise at the rarity and infrequency of it.'

Memoirs of Ambrose Barnes 1649

'This Man against whom the Lord hath witnessed.'
Cromwell to Colonel Hammond, 1648

31

Protect your lambs against cold and predators: cook wildfowl.

Young broom or good pasture thy ewes do require
Warm barn and in safety their lambs do desire
Look often well to them, for foxes and dogs
For pits and for brambles, for vermin and hogs.
Tusser *Five Hundred Points of Good Husbandry* 1573

'To boil a mallard curiously. Take the mallard when it is fair dressed, washed and trussed, and put it on a spit and roast it until you get the fat and gravy out of it. Then take it from the spit and boil it, and take the best of the broth into a pan: put to it the gravy which you saved, with a piece of sweet butter, currants, vinegar, pepper and grated bread. Thus boil all these together, and when the duck is boiled sufficiently, lay it on a dish with the broth upon it, and so serve it forth.'
Markham *The English Housewife* 1683

FEBRUARY

THE MONTH OF PURIFICATION

Named from Februa, the great Roman feast of purification.
In Welsh: *Chwefror*
In Gaelic: *Faoilleach* – the month of ravaging wolves.
In Anglo-Saxon: *Solmonath* – the month of cakes, now offered
to the gods.

1

St Brides' Day: Imbolc, the Celtic feast of Spring's awakening.

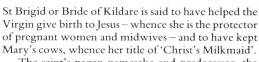

St Brigid or Bride of Kildare is said to have helped the Virgin give birth to Jesus – whence she is the protector of pregnant women and midwives – and to have kept Mary's cows, whence her title of 'Christ's Milkmaid'.

The saint's pagan namesake and predecessor, the Celtic goddess Brigit, was also associated with fertility, childbirth, and cattle. On her feast day – which is also the Gaelic spring festival of Imbolc – Highland girls made the 'Last Sheaf' of the previous harvest into images of her, which were laid in a decorated cradle called 'Bride's Bed'.

> This is the day of Bride
> The Queen will come from the Mound
> This is the day of Bride
> The serpent will come from the hole.

On this mystic day adders were believed to abandon their winter lairs: and the oyster-catcher birds – called in Gaelic *Gille Brighde*, 'the servants of Bride' – made their appearance, bringing Spring with them.

2

Candlemas: 'St Mary's Feast of the Candles', officially the Feast of the Purification and the Presentation of Christ in the Temple.

Forty days after Christ's birth, the Virgin Mary ritually cleansed herself and presented her child in the Temple at Jerusalem: there she met the aged Simeon, who prophesied that Jesus would be 'a light to lighten the Gentiles'. Today, therefore, lights and candles are blessed in churches, and candlelit services and processions are held.

> Candlemas Day, plant beans in the clay
> Put candles and candlesticks all away

By this season it has grown light enough to do most 'inside work' without candles.

> If Candlemas Day bring snow and rain
> Winter is gone, and won't come again
> If Candlemas Day be clear and bright
> Winter will have another flight

Fine weather today is to be feared, since it shows that the worst of winter is still to come.

> A good farmer should have, on Candlemas Day
> Half his turnips, and half his hay.

FEBRUARY

St Blaise's Day, or Blaze Day.

St Blaise was traditionally a Bishop of Sebaste in Armenia, who on his way to execution miraculously cured a boy who had a fishbone lodged in his throat. He is therefore invoked against all throat ailments.

On his day, some churches hold ceremonies of Blessing the Throats, when hallowed candles are tied into the shape of a cross and touched against the throats of sufferers.

'Good for the throat: Honey, sugar, butter with a little salt, liquorice, to sup soft eggs, hyssop, a mean manner of eating and drinking, and sugar candy. Evil for the throat: Mustard, much lying on the breast, pepper, anger, things roasted, lechery, much working, too much rest, much drink, smoke of incense, old cheese and all sour things are naughty for the throat.'
The Kalendar of Shepheardes 1604

February the Third is the earliest possible date of Shrove Tuesday.

The land needs rain this month, and snow is even more beneficial: snowdrops now blooming.

> Feb fill the dyke
> Either black or white
> But if with white, 'tis the better to like.
>
> If February gives much snow
> A fine summer it doth foreshow.
>
> If in February there fall no rain.
> 'Tis neither good for hay nor grain.

Snowdrops, also called Candlemas Bells, February Fair Maids, Snowbells and Snowpiercers, now bloom in many places: and Welsh border people gather bunches of them 'to purify the house'. Yet this may be risky, for Snowdrops are known as Death Flowers in some counties – perhaps because they grow in church-yards, and recall the white mourning worn for children – and there it is held dangerous to pick them.

5

St Agatha's Day: seek cures for sore breasts.

According to the legend of St Agatha, she was tortured by having her breasts cut off, and she is often shown carrying the severed organs on a platter. So she is invoked against breast disorders, and – because her breasts were mistaken for bells or loaves – is also the patroness of bellfounders and bakers.

'Whosoever shall take a Mole and hold her in his right hand till she die, shall have such an excellent Virtue therein, that he shall ease the pain of a woman's breasts only by touching them.'

Edward Topsell *History of Four-footed Beasts* 1607

6

**About Candlemas Day
Every good goose should lay.**

'It is observed of geese, that in case the waters are frozen up (as in some hard winters they are) about their treading time, then the most part of their eggs will prove addled. The reason is said to be because the goose proves more fruitful when she is trod by the gander on the water, than on the land.'

Worlidge *Systema Agriculturae* 1697

On this day in 1685, King Charles II died. During his lifetime, his crony Lord Rochester had written a satirical epitaph for him:

> Here lies our great and sovereign Lord
> Whose word no man relies on
> He never said a foolish thing
> Nor ever did a wise one.

To which Charles, however, replied: 'My words are my own, my actions are my ministers'.'

'Not long before the Death of King Charles II a Sparrow-Hawk escaped from the Perch, and pitched on one of the Iron Crowns of the White Tower, and entangling its string in the Crown, hung by the heels and died. Twas considered very ominous, and so it proved.'

John Aubrey *Miscellanies* 1695

FEBRUARY

7

This is the season of mass ball games: like the Candlemas and Shrove Tuesday 'Hurling' games of Cornwall.

'When they meet, there is neither comparing of numbers, or matching of men; but a silver ball is cast up and that company which can catch, and carry it by force or sleight to the place assigned, gaineth the ball and victory. The Hurlers take their next way over hills, dales, hedges, ditches, yea, and through bushes, briars, mires, plashes and rivers whatsoever: so as you shall sometimes see 20 or 30 lie tugging together in the water, scrambling and scratching for the ball. A play (verily) both rude and rough. . . . The ball in this play may be compared to an infernal spirit; for whosoever catcheth it, fareth straightways like a mad man, struggling and fighting with those that go about to hold him. . . . You shall see them retiring home as from a pitched battle, with bloody pates, bones broken and out of joint, and such bruises as serve to shorten their days: yet all is good play, and never Attorney or Coroner troubled.'

Carew *The Survey of Cornwall* 1602

8

Be careful of your health and diet.

'In this month all slimy fish, white meats, foggy fen-fowls, milk and such-like food of a phlegmatic humour, that do oppilate and stop the liver and veins and thicken the blood, are to be eschewed.'

Browne's *Almanack* 1627

'To make Tea with Eggs. The Jesuit that came from China, Anno 1664, told Mr Waller that there they sometimes use in this manner. To near a pint of the infusion of Tea, take two yolks of new-laid eggs, and beat them very well with a quantity of fine Sugar. When they are very well incorporated pour your Tea on the Eggs and Sugar, stir them well together, and so drink it hot. This is when you come home from attending business abroad, are very hungry, and yet have not conveniency to eat presently a competent meal: it flyeth suddenly through the whole body and into the veins, and strengtheneth exceedingly.'

The Closet of Sir Kenelm Digby Opened 1669

9

St Apollonia's Day: seek cures for toothache.

The historical St Apollonia, an aged Christian matron of Alexandria, had her teeth pulled out before her martyrdom: she is thus invoked against toothache, and is the protectress of dentists.

'A sure medicine for toothache. The grey worms breeding under wood or stones and having many feet, and when they be touched they do cluster together like porkenpicks. These pierced through with a bodkin and put into the tooth that acheth allayeth the pain.'
                    John Hollybush *The Homish Apothecary* 1561

'Take a new nail, and make the gum bleed with it, and then drive it into an oak. This did cure William Neal, a very stout Gentleman, when he was almost mad with the pain, and had a mind to have pistolled himself.'
                    John Aubrey *Miscellanies* 1695

10

Avoid travelling by night in snowy weather.

> For she was all froze in with frost
> Eight days and nights, poor soul
> But when they gave her up for lost
> They found her down the hole.

On this day in 1799 a passing farmer, noticing a handkerchief hanging on a bush, rescued Elizabeth Woodcock of Impington in Cambridgeshire from the snow hole in which she had taken refuge from a blizzard on the night of February the second. Drifting snow had subsequently covered her to a depth of six feet, and she had become too weak to climb out: during her confinement her only sustenance was two pinches of snuff.

> Walk fast in snow
> In frost walk slow
> When frost and snow are both together
> Sit by the fire and save shoe leather.

The best time of the year to breed dogs: foxes also now mating.

11

'You shall put your Dog and Bitch together to engender and breed either in January, February, or March, according as they grow proud: and you shall not forget to observe, that when your Bitch be limed the Moon is either in Aquarius or Gemini. For the whelps which are engendered under those signs will never run mad: and, for the most part, the litter will have at least double so many Dog-whelps as Bitch-whelps.'

Markham *Country Contentments* 1615

'Foxes begin now to be very rank, and to smell so high, that as one rides along of a morning it is easy to distinguish where they have been. At this season the intercourse between the sexes commences; and the females intimate their wants to the males by three or four little sharp yelpings or barkings frequently repeated.'

Journals of Gilbert White February 1778

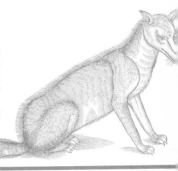

Alder-tree catkins now beginning to appear in most years.

12

'Alder is of all other the most faithful lover of watery and boggy places. The shadow of this tree does feed and nourish the very grass that grows under it; and being set and well plashed, it is an excellent defence to the banks of rivers. The wood is likewise useful . . . for such building and works as lie continually under water, where it will harden like a stone.'

John Evelyn *Sylva* 1664

> Alder for shoes
> Do wise men choose

Being water-resistant and heat-retaining, alder is the best wood for clog soles.

'Alder leaves gathered while the morning dew is on them, and brought into a chamber troubled with fleas, will gather them thereunto: which being suddenly cast out, will rid the chamber of these troublesome bedfellows.'

Culpeper *Herbal* 1653

13

Valentine's Eve: draw lots for Valentines.

To draw lots on Valentine's Eve, as it is done in northern England and the southern part of Scotland. Let an equal number of maids and bachelors assemble together, and let each person's name be written on a slip of paper, the boys' slips being placed in one bag and the girls' in the other. Each boy then draws a slip from the girls' bag, and each girl one from the boys', the name drawn being the Valentine. Thus everyone has two Valentines to choose between, yet will generally prefer the one he or she draws to the one that has drawn them; but should John draw Joan, and Joan happen also to draw John, then the couple will surely marry. Sometimes every boy and girl draws thrice, putting the slip back into the bag after the first and second times: and if the same name be drawn thrice, this also is a certain prognostic of matrimony.

Before you go to bed, write the names of any prospective lovers on slips of paper, roll the slips in clay balls, and drop these into a bowl of water. The first to rise to the surface will be your Valentine tomorrow.

14

**Oft have I heard both youths and virgins say
Birds choose their mates, and couple too,**
> **today**

**But by their flight I never can divine
When I shall couple with my Valentine**
Herrick *Hesperides* 1648

The tradition that birds pair off today (which is of unknown origin, but which is approximately true for some species) seems to have been the reason why February the fourteenth became the great lovers' festival: certainly the two obscure Saints Valentine commemorated today have nothing to do with romance.

The first person of the opposite sex you see today – excepting your family – must be your Valentine: but it is permissible to keep your eyes shut until the right person appears.

Sow early plants: and protect them with a Hot Bed.

15

'In February, in the New of the Moon, sow Borage, Coriander, Marjoram, Radish, Rosemary and Sorrel.'
Markham *The English Housewife* 1683

'To make a hot Bed in February, for the raising of any tender Plants or Flowers, you must provide a warm place defended from all Winds by a Pale made of Reed or Straw, about six feet high: within which you must raise a Bed of about two or three foot high and three foot across, of new horse-dung, treading it very hard down on the top, level. Lay on this of fine rich mould about three or four inches thick: and when the extreme heat of the Bed is over (which you may perceive by thrusting in your finger) then plant your seeds. Then erect some forks four or five inches above the Bed, to support a frame of sticks covered in straw, to defend the plants from cold and wet: only you may open your covering on a warm day for an hour before and an hour after noon.'
Worlidge *Systema Agriculturae* 1697

Lent, the season of forty days fasting before Easter, generally begins in February: but because Easter is a 'movable feast', dependent on the phases of the Moon, the date of Lent's beginning is also variable, ranging from February the fourth to March the tenth.

16

Lent's English name comes from the Anglo-Saxon *lenctene* – meaning the time when the days lengthen – but in Scotland it is 'Fasterns', and its Gaelic and Welsh names also mean 'the fast'. In Latin, more precisely, it is *carnisprivium*, the time of abstinence from meat, in memory of Christ's forty-day fast in the Wilderness.

Whenever it begins, Lent is always preceded by Shrovetide, the season when people made their pre-Lent 'shrifts' or confessions. At this time, too, all meat and other foods forbidden in Lent had to be eaten up, so that an atmosphere of last-minute feasting and carnival (from the Latin *carnelevarium* – 'the taking away of meat') prevailed.

17

During the week which ended on this day in 1719, the following diseases and conditions proved fatal to the inhabitants of London.

Abortive	2	The Imposthume	2
Aged	49	Measles	9
Asthma	2	Mortification	2
Canker	1	Rising in the Lights	5
Child-bed	6	The Small Pox	55
Chrisoms	1	Sore Leg	1
Colick	2	Stillborn	15
Consumption	50	Stoppage in the	
Convulsions	139	Stomach	5
Dropsie	28	Suddenly	4
The King's Evil	2	Of their Teeth	43
Fever	51	Thrush	1
The French Pox	2	The Tissick	8
Gout	1	Twisting in The Guts	2
Griping in the Guts	20	Tympany	1
Headmouldshot	2	Worms	1
Jaundies	3	Executed	4

The London Bills of Mortality, 1719

18

Finish up meat supplies before Lent comes: ravens now nesting.

Shrove Monday – the Monday before the beginning of Lent, and immediately preceding Shrove Tuesday – is called 'Collop Monday' in the North of England, because the meat forbidden during the coming fast was then consumed in the form of 'collops' or 'rashers'. Generally these were of bacon, eaten now with eggs: but mutton collops were also much favoured.

The ill-omened raven, one of the first British birds to nest, should by now be hatching eggs.

Coltsfoot flowers now appearing in most years: destroy molehills, except in wet pastureland.

19

So called because of the shape of its leaves – which appear *after* the flowers, hence its northern nickname of 'Son-afore-the-Father' – coltsfoot is also called 'Poor Man's Baccy' and still used in herbal smoking mixtures.

'The fume of the dried leaves [of coltsfoot] taken through a funnel . . . effectually helpeth those that are troubled with coughs and shortness of breath, and fetch their wind thick and often. Being taken in manner as they take Tobacco, it mightily prevaileth.'
Gerard *Herbal* 1633

Get mole-catcher cunningly moles for to kill
And harrow and cast abroad every hill
If pasture by nature is given to be wet
Then bear with the molehills, though thick they be set
That lamb may sit on it, and so to sit dry
Or else to lie by it, the warmer to lie.
Tusser *Five Hundred Points of Good Husbandry* 1573

The Sun enters the House of Pisces.

20

'The man born under Pisces shall be a great goer, a fornicater, a mocker, and covetous: he will say one thing and do another. He shall trust in his sapience, he shall have good fortune: he will be a defender of widows and orphans. He shall be fearful on water: he shall soon pass all adversities and live seventy-two years after nature.

'The woman shall be delicious, familiar in jests, pleasant of courage, fervent, a great drinker. She shall have sickness of her eyes and be sorrowful by shame, needlessly. Her husband will leave her, and she shall have much trouble with strangers. She shall travel much, have pain in her stomach, and live seventy-seven years.

'Both man and woman shall live faithfully.'
Kalendar of Shepheardes 1604

21

Observe the feet, which are governed by Pisces: and be careful how you put on your shoes.

'The feet short and thick, signifieth a person to be weak; slender and short, to be wicked; fleshy and hard, to be a blockhead. The feet small and fair-formed, to be a fornicater; much hairy, to be lecherous and bold; naked of hair, to be weak of strength and courage; the inner part of the sole, not hollow but filled with flesh, that they make no hollowness in the step, to be beyond measure crafty and cunning.'

The Shepherd's Prognostication 1729

It is considered most unlucky to put, by mistake, the right foot into the left shoe, or vice-versa: and also, some say, to put on the left shoe before the right when dressing. Putting on a sock or stocking inside-out, however, is very fortunate: but only if it is done by accident.

Setting out on any journey, put your 'best' (which is to say your right) 'foot forward'.

22

But hark, I hear the Pancake Bell
The fritters make a gallant smell
Poor Robin's Almanack 1684

'To make fine pancakes fried without butter or lard. Take a pint of cream and six new-laid eggs, beat them very well together, put in a quarter of a pound of sugar and one nutmeg grated or a little mace (which you please) and so much flour as will thicken as much as ordinary Pancake batter. Your pan must be heated reasonable hot and wiped with a clean cloth: this done, put in the batter as thick or thin as you please.'

The Compleat Cook 1671

FEBRUARY

The first day of Lent, immediately following Shrove Tuesday whenever it falls, is solemn Ash Wednesday – so called from the ashes then smeared on the foreheads of churchgoers, to remind them that 'they are but dust, and to dust shall return'. The ashes used are traditionally those of last year's Palm Sunday palms.

23

The traditional season for playing marbles begins on Ash Wednesday and ends on Good Friday. As played in Surrey and Sussex, forty-nine marbles are thrown at random onto a six-foot diameter ring: and players compete in turn to knock as many as possible out, using a 'shooting marble' called the 'tolley'. This is flicked with the thumb only, keeping the hand stationary, with the first finger 'knuckled down' to the ground.

St Matthias's Day: coppice woodland for fuel.

24

St Matthias, 'the thirteenth apostle', was traditionally beheaded with an axe, and is thus the patron of carpenters and woodcutters.

'Fell coppice and fuel to burn, where you would have the root to spring forth new supplies, in February or March: and in the first week of the Moon's age.'
Luke's *Almanack* 1627

On Saint Matthi
Put candlesticks by

The days are now very perceptibly becoming longer: but, 'If it freeze on St Matthias's Day, it will freeze for two months together' – at least in Scotland.

25

The first violets – the Sweet, Scented, or Purple variety – flower about now in sheltered places.

'Violets have great prerogative above others, not only because the mind conceiveth a certain pleasure and recreation by smelling and handling these most odoriferous flowers, but also for that very many by these violets receive ornament and comely grace: for there be made of them garlands for the head, nosegays and posies, which are delightful to look on and pleasant to smell to.'

Gerard *Herbal* 1633

'To make Oil of Violets: which, if it be rubbed about the Temples, assuageth the headache, provoketh sleep, and moisteneth the brain; and it is good against melancholy, dullness, and heaviness of spirit. Take salad oil and put it in an earthenware pot: then take fresh Violet leaves, clip off all the white and bruise them a little, and put them in the oil. Then stop the pot close, set it into a boiling pan of water, and let it boil one hour. Then let it stand all night on hot embers or a small fire: the next day take the oil and strain from it the leaves: put it into a glass, and put therein good store of fresh Violet leaves clipt as before. Stop it, and set it in the Sun every day for a fortnight or three weeks: then you may use it.'

Thomas Jenner *The Book of Fruits and Flowers* 1653

26

Set hens now for spring chickens.

'The best time to set Hens to have the best, largest and most kindly Chickens, is in February, in the increase of the Moon, so that she may hatch or disclose her Chickens in the increase of the next new Moon, being in March: for one brood of March chickens is worth three broods of any other. A Hen will cover nineteen eggs well, but upon what number soever you set her, let it be odd. Mark the upper side of them, and then watch the Hen to see if she busy herself to turn them from one side to the other: which if you see she doth not . . . you must supply that office.'

Markham *Cheap and Good Husbandry* 1613

If hard weather continues, beware of taking cold: protect your provisions from hungry mice.

'Of this wise ought they to be bathed dry which have taken cold, before they do bath in water. Take mugwort, sage, fennel, pennyroyal of each a handful: chop them small and put them in two bags, and seeth them. Then put the water the herbs have been sodden in into a tub, and set thy feet therein as hot as ye can suffer it. Lay one of the bags under and sit thereupon: and lay the other upon your stomach reaching down to your privy members. But look the bags be not too hot.'

John Hollybush *The Homish Apothecary* 1561

'To drive away Mice. If the brains of a Weasel be sprinkled upon Cheese or any other meat whereto Mice resort, they not only forbear to eat thereof, but also to come nigh that place.'
Edward Topsell *The History of Four Footed Beasts* 1607

The bad weather usual now produces much talk round the fire: mind your conversation.

'And they do as much amiss that never have any other thing in their mouth, than their children, their wife, and their nurse: "My little boy made me so to laugh yesterday, hear you, you never saw a sweeter babe in your life." "My wife is such a one: of a truth you would not believe what a wit she hath." For it irks a man's ears to hearken to it. Neither follow those, that show themselves so afraid and fearful to speak their minds, when a man doth ask their advice, with so much fetching about ere they come to their matter, that it is deadly pain to hear them: "Sir, I beseech you pardon me, If I do not say well. And Sir, I am sure you will but mock me for it. But yet, to obey you." '
Robert Peterson *Treatise of Manners and Behaviours* 1564

29

Leap Year's Day or Job's Birthday: a hazardous day for single men.

February the twenty-ninth occurs only once every four years, in leap years: its addition being designed to rectify the discrepancy between the calendar year of 365 days and the solar year of approximately $365\frac{1}{4}$ days.

Leap years are regarded as generally unlucky in Scotland, and Leap Year's Day is particularly ill-omened: this is said to be because it was Job's birthday, which the prophet blighted when he 'cursed the day he was born'. In His mercy, however, the Lord only allows it to occur every four years.

'Ladies have a full and absolute license to propose marriage to single gentlemen on February the 29th: and if the gentleman is so rude as to refuse, he is infallibly bound to give the spurned lady a present, which is usually a pair of new gloves on Easter Day.'

The Arbiter of Polite Comportment 1710

MARCH

THE MONTH OF NEW LIFE

Named after Mars, the Roman God of War.
In Welsh: *Mawrth*
In Gaelic: *Mart*, or *Earrach Geamraidh* – 'the Winter Spring'.
In Anglo-Saxon: *Hrethamonath* – the month of the goddess Hretha.

1

Gwyl Dewi Sant, the Feast of St David, patron saint of Wales: in whose memory leeks are worn today.

Some say, however, that the leek-wearing custom commemorates a great Welsh victory over the Saxons, or that it is favoured because its white and green colours are those of the Welsh flag.

Eat leeks in March, and ramsons [wild garlic] in May
And all the year after physicians may play.

'The leek breedeth wind, and evil juice, and maketh heavy dreams; it stirreth a man to make water, and is good for the belly: but if you will boil a leek in two waters and afterwards steep it in cold water, it will be less windy than it was before. The use of leeks is good for them that would have childer.'

William Turner Herbal 1568

If from fleas you would be free
On March the First, let doors and windows closed be.

This is traditionally the day when 'the black soldiers' invade houses.

2

St Chad's Day: eggs now becoming plentiful.

By Valentine's Day
Every good hen, duck or goose should lay
By David and Chad
Every hen, duck or goose should lay, good or bad.

'If you feed your Hens often with toasts taken out of ale, or with barley boiled, they will lay soon. Now because eggs of themselves are a singular profit, you shall understand that the best way to preserve or keep them long is some think to lay them in straw, but that is too cold, and besides will make them musty; others will lay them in bran, but that will make them putrefy: and others lay them in salt, but that makes them diminish. The best way then to keep them most sweet, sound and full, is only to keep them in a heap of malt, close and well covered all over.'

Markham Cheap and Good Husbandry 1613

To brawle for Gaine, the Cocke *doth ſleight;*
But, for his Females, *he will fight.*

MARCH

St Winnold's Day: look out for rough weather: Shrove Tuesday falls about now when Easter is late.

3

> First comes David
> Next comes Chad
> Then comes Winnold, roaring like mad.

Windy and stormy weather is seasonable and to be expected during these first three days of March: and if it does not come now, it is saving itself for the three 'Borrowing Days' at the month's end.

'To make Pancakes so crisp that you may set them upright. Make a dozen or a score of them in a little frying pan, not bigger than a saucer: and then boil them in lard, and they will look as yellow as gold, besides the taste.'

The Newe Book of Cookerie 1615

Manure your garden: and marry if you dare.

4

'Pigeons' or hens' dung is incomparable for the garden, one load being worth ten loads of any other dung. I have known a quince tree whereon poultry always perched, that by reason of the rain washing to its roots the salt and fatness of the dung, did bear yearly an incredible number of very fat quinces.'

Worlidge *Systema Agriculturae* 1697

> Marry in March when born in June
> Then you're sure to win the croun.
> North-east Scotland

5

Mad March hares – the most mysterious and sacred of British animals – now performing their mating rituals.

'The common sort of people suppose that hares are one year male and one year female . . . yet hunters object that there be some which are only females and no more; but no male that is not also a female, and so they make him an hermaphrodite.'

Edward Topsell *History of Four-footed Beasts* 1607

It is specially unlucky to meet a hare when setting out on a journey, or to mention one by name before putting out to sea: if you must then speak of hares, use a nickname like 'Wat' or 'Old Malkin'.

Hares acting oddly may well be shape-shifting witches or 'were-hares', and as such can only be killed with a silver bullet, or by placing rowan and vervain behind the gun-stock.

6

Take good care of your lute, especially in damp weather.

'That you may know how to shelter your Lute, in the worst of Ill Weathers (which is moist) you shall do well, ever when you Lay it by in the daytime, to put it into a Bed, that is constantly used, between the Rug and the Blanket; but never between the Sheets, because they may be moist with Sweat, etcetera. A Bed will secure it from all Inconveniences, and keep your Glue so Hard as Glass, and all safe and sure; only to be excepted. That no Person be so inconsiderate, as to Tumble down upon the Bed whilst the Lute is there. For I have known several Good Lutes spoiled with such a Trick.'

Thomas Mace *Musick's Monument* 1676

Do not despise the young stinging nettles now beginning to appear: for they have many uses.

7

'Nettle tops are usually boiled in pottage in the Spring time, to consume the Phlegmatic superfluities in the body of man, that the coldness and moistness of the winter hath left behind. And it is said that if the juice of the roots of nettles be mixed with ale and beer, and given to one that is suspected to have lost her maidenhood, if it remain with her she is a maid, but if she spew it forth she is not.'

William Coles *Adam in Eden* 1657

To make nettle beer. Take a gallon measure of freshly gathered young nettles, washed, well dried and well packed down. Boil them in a gallon of water for at least a quarter of an hour. Then strain them, press them and put the juice in an earthenware pot with a pound of brown sugar and the juice and grated skin of a lemon. Stir well, and before it grows cool put in an ounce of yeast dissolved in some of the liquid. Cover with a cloth, and leave in a warm place for four or five days: then strain again and bottle it, stopping the bottles well. It will be ready after a week, but better if left longer.

Sow garden herbs and water them: but hope for a dry, dusty month to benefit the crops.

8

In March and in April, from morning to night
In sowing and setting, good housewives delight
To have in a garden, or other like plot
To physic their house, or to furnish their pot.

Tusser *Five Hundred Points of Good Husbandry* 1573

'In March, the Moon being new, sow Garlic, Chervil, Marjoram, white Poppy, double Marigolds, Thyme and Violets. At the full Moon, Chicory, Fennel, and Apples of Love. At the wane, Artichokes, Basil, Cucumbers, Spinach, Gillyflowers, Cabbage, Lettuce, Burnets, Leeks and Savory.'

Markham *The English Housewife* 1683

March damp and warm
Doth the farmer much harm
But a March without water
Dowers the farmer's daughter

9 Exercise and divert yourself by dancing: but be careful.

'Dancing, or saltation, is both a pleasant and a profitable art, which confers and preserves health: it is proper to youth, agreeable to the old, and suitable for all, provided fitness of time and place are observed. . . . And it is a useful device for ascertaining whether a person be deformed by the gout . . . or if they emit an unpleasant odour, as of bad meat.'

Arbeau *Orchésographie* 1588

'What clipping, what culling, what kissing and bussing, what smouching and slobbering of one another, what filthy groping and unclean handling is not practised everywhere in these dancings? And whereas they conclude it is a wholesome exercise for the body, the contrary is most true: for I have known divers, by the immoderate use thereof, have in a short time become decrepit and lame. Some have broke their legs with skipping, leaping, turning and vaulting, and some have come by one hurt, some by another: but never any came thence without some part of his mind broken and lame.'

Philip Stubbes *The Anatomy of Abuses* 1576

10 The latest possible date of Ash Wednesday and the beginning of the Lenten fast.

Is this a Fast, to keep
   The larder lean
     And clean
From fat of veals and sheep?

Is it to quit the dish
   Of flesh, yet still
     To fill
The platter high with fish?

No; 'tis a Fast to dole
   Thy sheaf of wheat
     And meat
Unto the hungry soul.

It is to fast from strife
   From old debate
     And hate
To circumcise thy life.

Herrick *Noble Numbers* 1647

'Penny Loaf Day' at Newark: heed the warnings revealed in dreams.

On the night of the 11th of March 1644, during the Civil War siege of Newark in Nottinghamshire by the forces of Parliament, Hercules Clay of that town dreamt three times in succession that his house was on fire. Twice he ignored the warning, and went back to sleep: but after the third dream he led his family out of the house – which was, sure enough, very soon afterwards hit by an enemy 'bombshell'. In gratitude for his miraculous deliverance, Clay bequeathed sufficient money to finance a distribution of 'penny loaves' to the Newark poor on its anniversary, and for a commemorative sermon which is still preached on or about this date.

St Gregory's Day.

St Gregory the Great, who died on this day in 604, was the Pope who sent St Augustine to convert the Anglo-Saxons. According to Bede, he was moved to this action by an encounter in the Roman slave market with some fair-haired English captives. On being told that they were Angles, he replied 'not Angles, but Angels' and on hearing that they came from Deira in Northumbria, he retorted that he would save them from the wrath (*de ira* in Latin) of God. And finally, when informed that their king's name was 'Aella', the relentless ecclesiastical punster rejoined that Christian 'Alleluias' would soon be heard in their land.

13

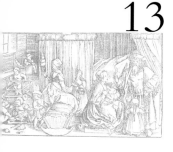

Mothering Sunday falls about now when Easter comes in early April.

> On Mothering Sunday, above all other
> Every child should dine with its mother.

Mothering Sunday – also called Mid-Lent Sunday – is the fourth Sunday in Lent, when the Epistle refers to 'Jerusalem, the mother of us all'. Perhaps for that reason, it has long been traditional – as at Worcester in 1644, for 'all the children and grandchildren to meet at the head and chief of the family and have a feast': and for children living away from home to visit their mothers 'and make them a present of money, a trinket, or some nice eatable'. Flowers – especially violets – are now the usual Mothering Sunday present.

> I'll to thee a Simnel bring
> 'Gainst thou goest a–Mothering
> So that, when she blesseth thee
> Half that blessing thou'lt give me.
>
> Herrick *Hesperides* 1647

Simnels were the customary 'Mothering Cakes' and are still popular. One way to make them is to beat together four ounces of butter and four ounces of brown sugar, adding two eggs one at a time. Then stir in six ounces of plain flour, half a teaspoon of baking powder, two ounces of dried fruit, orange juice and some grated orange peel. Put all this in a well-greased cake tin, and cover it with four ounces of almond paste shaped to the tin: then bake it slowly for two and a half hours.

14

Blue-purple Periwinkle and yellow Lesser Celandine – or Pilewort – now flowering.

'It is a tradition with many, that a wreath made of Periwinkle and bound about the legs, defendeth them from cramp . . . a friend of mine, who was very vehemently tormented with the cramp, could be by no means eased, till he had wrapped some of the branches hereof about his legs. And Mr Culpeper writeth, that Periwinkle leaves eaten by man and wife together cause love – which is a rare quality indeed, if it be true.'

William Coles *Adam in Eden* 1657

The Roman Ides of March: beware weasels and other ill omens.

15

'The Bust of King Charles I carved by Bernini, as it was brought in a Boat upon the Thames, a strange Bird (the like whereof the Bargemen had never seen) dropped a drop of Blood or Blood-like upon it: which left a stain not to be wiped off.'

John Aubrey *Miscellanies* 1695

'They hold opinion in England, that if they meet with a Weasel in the morning, that they shall not speed well that day. There is nothing in this beast more strange, than their conception and generation: for Weasels do not couple in their hinder parts, but at their Ears, and bring forth their young at their mouths. Yet it is certain that they have places of conception under their tails: and therefore how it should come to pass that their young ones should come out of their mouths, I cannot easily learn.'

Edward Topsell *History of Four-footed Beasts* 1607

March kittens – the best kind of cat – now being born.

16

'During the time of copulation, the female cat continually crieth, whereof the writers give a double cause: one, because she is pinched with the talons of the male in the time of his lustful rage: and the other, because his seed is so fiery hot, that it almost burneth the female's place of conception. When they have kittened they rage against dogs, and will suffer none to come near their young ones. The best to keep are such as are littered in March.'

Edward Topsell *History of Four-footed Beasts* 1607

'Cats were anciently revered as Emblems of the Moon, and among the Egyptians had stately Temples erected to their honour. It is said that in whatever House a Cat died, all the Family shaved their Eye-brows.'

Brand *Observations of Popular Antiquities* 1813

'The Cat, by putting her Foot over her Ear when washing her face, foreshows Rain.'

Worlidge *Systema Agriculturae* 1697

17

St Patrick's Day.

St Patrick (d.461) is said to have used his symbol, the three-leaved shamrock, to illustrate the doctrine of the Trinity, and to have banished all snakes from Ireland.

The identity of St Patrick's shamrock – the Irish *seamrog*, or 'little clover' – is much disputed: some say it was really Wood Sorrel, but the plant worn by Irishmen everywhere today is the Lesser Yellow Trefoil. Shamrock – or any kind of clover – with four or five leaves is an especially lucky charm: but only if it is found by chance rather than searched for.

In the Highlands and Islands of Scotland, where Patrick is as much honoured as in Ireland, his feast is hailed as the first day of Spring. In the Hebrides a south wind is expected this morning, bringing the saint to visit his parishioners: and a north wind in the evening, to bear him back to Ireland.

'On the high day of Patrick, every fold will have a cow-calf, and every pool a salmon.'

Gaelic saying

18

March chickens now hatching: make Cock Ale with a lucky March cockerel.

Keep a black cock hatched in March as a protection against evil spirits: his crowing terrifies them.

'To make Cock Ale. Take eight gallons of Ale; then take a March Cock and boil him well; and take four pounds of raisins well stoned, two or three nutmegs, three or four flakes of mace and half a pound of dates. Beat all these in a mortar, and put to them two quarts of the best sherry-sack. Put all this into the Ale, with the Cock, and stop it close six or seven days, and then bottle it: and after a month you may drink it.'

The Closet of Sir Kenelm Digby Opened 1669

MARCH

St Joseph's Day: children born today will be lucky, but take care how they are baptized.

Children born today are most fortunate: and according to a Highland belief they cannot be shot in battle.

'Within these last seven years, the Minister has been twice interrupted in administering Baptism to a female child before the male child, who was baptized immediately after. When the service was over, he was gravely told he had done very wrong: for, as the female child was first baptized, she would on her coming to the years of discretion, most certainly have a strong beard, and the boy would have none.'
Old Statistical Account, South Ronaldsay, Orkney, 1795

A clear St Joseph's Day presages a fine and fertile year.

Carlings Sunday falls about now when Easter comes in early April.

> Ted, med, miseray
> Carlings, Palm and Pace-Egg Day.

The fifth Sunday in Lent, generally called 'Passion Sunday' because Christ's sufferings are then remembered, is called 'Care' ('mourning') or 'Carlings Sunday' in north-eastern England and Scotland, and 'Sul y Pys' (Peas Sunday) in Wales. Probably because of a misinterpretation of 'Passion Sunday' as 'Peasen Sunday', dried peas (or 'carlings') prepared in various ways are the traditional dish on this day.

In Scotland and Northumberland, carling peas are first soaked in water overnight, then fried in butter and eaten with salt and pepper, or with sugar and rum. Alternatively (as in Wales) they may be steeped in wine or cider instead of water; or, as on Teesside, boiled with fat bacon instead of being fried, and then eaten cold with vinegar.

21

The Spring Equinox, and the First Day of Spring: the Sun enters the House of Aries.

'He that is born in Aries shall be of good wit, and neither rich nor poor. He shall be soon angry and soon pleased. He shall have damage by his neighbours, he shall have power over dead folks' goods. He shall be a liar, and unsteadfast of courage, and will take vengeance on his enemies. Unto thirty-four years he shall be a fornicater, and wedded at thirty-five: and if he be not, he shall not be chaste. He shall have great sickness at twenty-two years, and if he escape he shall live seventy-five years after nature.

'The woman that is born in this time shall be ireful, and suffer great wrongs from day to day. She shall lose her husband and recover a better. She shall be sick at five years, and in danger at twenty-five, and if she escape, she shall be in doubt until forty-three years, but afterwards prosper.'

Kalendar of Shepheardes 1604

22

Observe the features of the face, which are ruled by Aries: and seek cures for ills of the nose.

'The nose round, with a sharpness at the end, signifies one to be wavering of mind; the nose wholly crooked, to be unshamefaced and unstable; crooked like an eagle's beak, to be bold. The nose flat, to be lecherous and hasty in wrath; the nostrils large, to be ireful.'

The Shepherd's Prognostication 1729

'Arise Evans had a fungous Nose and said, it was revealed to him, that the King's hand would cure him. At the first coming of Charles II into St James's Park he kissed the King's hand and rubbed his Nose with it: which disturbed the King, but cured him.'

John Aubrey *Miscellanies* 1695

Lenten fish dishes still in demand.

23

'How to stew a Trout. Take a large Trout fair trimmed, and wash it, and put it into a deep pewter dish, then take half a pint of sweet wine, with a lump of butter and a little whole mace, parsley, savory, and thyme, mince them all small, and put them into the Trout's belly, and so let it stew a quarter of an hour. Then mince the yolk of an hard egg and strew it on the Trout, lay the herbs about it, scrape on sugar, and so serve it forth.'

Markham *The English Housewife* 1683

St Gabriel's Day: Queen Elizabeth died, 1603.

24

Gabriel the Archangel, who revealed to the Virgin Mary that she was to bear Jesus, is invoked today by all those who hope for good news; and he is the special protector of postmen and other messengers.

Early in the morning of March the twenty-fourth, 1603, Queen Elizabeth died at Richmond Palace near London: and the courtier Sir Robert Carey, determined to be the first to bring the news to her successor King James, set off on his epic ride to Edinburgh: 'I took horse between nine and ten o'clock; and that night rode to Doncaster. The Friday night I came to my own house at Witherington, and presently took order with my deputies to see the Borders kept in quiet; which they had much to do; and gave order the next morning, the King of Scotland should be proclaimed King of England. Very early on Saturday I took horse for Edinburgh, and came to Norham about twelve at noon, so that I might well have been with the King at supper time. But I got a great fall by the way; and my horse gave me a great blow on the head, that made me shed much blood. It made me so weak, that I was forced to ride a soft pace after; so that the King was nearly gone to bed by the time I knocked at the gate. I was quickly let in; and carried up to the King's Chamber, where I kneeled by him, and saluted him by his title of "England, Scotland, France and Ireland".'

Sir Robert Carey *Memoirs*, before 1627

25

Lady Day: the first day of the year, Old Style.

'Lady Day', or the Feast of the Annunciation, commemorates the Archangel Gabriel's proclamation to the Virgin Mary that she would bear Christ exactly nine months later, on Christmas Day. From the twelfth century until the calendar change of 1752 the twenty-fifth of March (and not the first of January) was the day on which the 'year of grace' began in England and Ireland. Thus (for example) March the twenty-fourth 1600 was immediately followed by March the twenty-fifth 1601: and an event recorded by contemporaries as happening on January the thirtieth 1648 took place according to modern reckoning on January the thirtieth 1649.

> When Easter falls in Our Lady's lap
> Then let England beware a rap.

Years when Easter Day coincides with Lady Day are said to be particularly ominous for England: this coincidence occurred in 1554 (when Queen Mary married Philip of Spain) and in 1649 (when Charles I was executed).

26

March hares now breeding.

'The Hare is a simple creature, having no defence but to run away, yet it is subtle . . . for she keepeth not her young ones together in one litter, but layeth them a furlong from one another, that she may not lose them all if peradventure men or beasts light on them.'
Edward Topsell *History of Four-footed Beasts* 1607

To carry a hare's foot is very lucky – but only if it contains jointed bones – and is a sovereign remedy against gout, stomach pains and insomnia.

'It is found by Experience that when one keeps a Hare alive and feedeth him, till he have occasion to eat him, if he tells him before he kills him, that he will do so, the hare will thereupon be found dead, having killed himself.'
John Aubrey *Remains of Gentilism* 1688

MARCH

Palm Sunday falls in late March when Easter comes in early April.

27

On Palm Sunday, the Sunday before Easter Day, the Church remembers Christ's triumphant entry into Jerusalem, when branches (traditionally of palm trees) were strewn in His path; and on this day palm crosses are blessed, distributed, and sometimes carried in procession.

True palm not being easily obtainable in Britain, other kinds of early-flowering greenery – and particularly catkinned branches of 'Pussy Willow' or 'English Palm' – were used instead for Palm Sunday decorations: and in many places young people went 'a-Palming' before dawn, returning at daybreak bearing willow boughs and wearing willow-catkins in their hats. This custom, however, was not exclusively a pious observance: and (as Aubrey remarked) 'this day gives many a Conception'.

Palm (or 'English Palm') crosses blessed on Palm Sunday should be carefully preserved, for they will protect the house from evil all the year.

28

When March is dry, seek remedies for difficult childbirths.

'A windy and a dry March is good for corn, but evil for old folks and child-bearing women.'

Dove's *Almanack* 1627

'If a woman have a strong and hard labour, take four spoonfuls of another woman's milk, and give it the woman to drink in her labour, and she shall be delivered presently.'

Markham *The English Housewife* 1683

'For the speedy delivery of women in child bed. Take the liver of an Eel killed in the full of the Moon (by reason the Moon hath such a very great influence over women). Dry it in the light of the Moon as much as possible you can without moulding: then in the Sun. Then bruise it to a fine powder and give it to the party in white wine: it will ease her pain.'

Mary William's Book, 1656

29

The first of the Borrowing Days: Mothering Sunday falls in this week when Easter is late.

The last three days of the month, which are often cold and stormy, are said to have been 'borrowed' by March from April.

> March borrowed from April
> Three days, and they were ill
> The first was snow and sleet
> The next was cold and weet
> The third was sic a freeze
> The birds' nebs stuck to trees.

'To roast mutton with oysters, for Mothering Sunday dinner. Take a shoulder of good mutton, and half a peck of oysters well washed and drained: then take the tops of rosemary, thyme and parsley chopped small, and the yolks of three hard eggs and an onion minced alltogether, and put thereto a quantity of gross pepper and four spoons of wine vinegar. Mingle all these with your oysters, and stuff all into the mutton. Set it in the oven and baste it with sweet butter: and when it is roasted put four spoons of white wine vinegar to the gravy and so serve it.'

Fairfax Household Book, 17th/18th century

Badger cubs now beginning to appear above ground.

30

'The badger diggeth her a den or cave in the earth and there liveth, never coming forth but for meat or easement, which she maketh out of her den. When they dig their den, after they have entered a good depth, one of them falleth on the back, and the other layeth all the earth on his belly, and so taketh his hinder feet in his mouth, and draweth the belly-laden badger out of the cave. He hath very sharp teeth, and is therefore accounted a deep-biting beast: his legs (as some say) are longer on the right side than the left, and therefore he runneth best when he getteth to the side of an hill.'

Edward Topsell *History of Four-footed Beasts* 1607

The common but valuable blue Ground Ivy – alias Gill-go-by-the-hedge, alias Alehoof – now beginning to flower: end this and every month luckily.

31

'Ground Ivy is commended against the humming noise and ringing sound of the ears, being put into them, and for them that are hard of hearing.'

Gerard *Herbal* 1633

It is lucky to say 'Hares, Hares' aloud as you go to bed on the last day of the month: and to say 'Rabbits, Rabbits' as soon as you awaken the following morning.

APRIL

THE SPRING CUCKOO'S MONTH

The Roman *Aperilis* – from *aperio*, to open or display: the month
when the Earth opens.
In Welsh: *Ebrill*
In Gaelic: *Ceitein na h-oinsich* – the cuckoo's May; the fool's May.
In Anglo-Saxon: *Eostramonath* – the month of the dawn goddess Eostra.

A Sive, of shelter maketh show;
But ev'ry Storme will through it goe.

APRIL

All Fools' Day, or 'Hunt the Gowk Day'.

1

On this ancient feast, of unknown origin, the most time-honoured method of making 'April Fools' is to send them on pointless errands: and articles much in request by victims include pigeons' milk, striped paint, copies of 'The Life of Eve's Mother', elbow grease, hens' teeth, and 'a long stand'.

> Don't you laugh and don't you smile
> Hunt the gowk another mile.

Bearing a sealed envelope containing this message, Scots 'gowks' (or 'April cuckoos') are today passed from one prankster to the next, each of whom thinks up a new errand and 'hunts the gowk' on.

'Yesterday being the first of April, several persons were sent to the Tower Ditch to see the lions washed.'
Dawks' *News-letter* 1698

> Twelve o'clock is past and gone
> You're the fool for making me one.

St Urban's Day: take April purges, and pray for beautiful hair.

2

> This April, with his stormy showers
> Doth make the earth yield pleasant flowers
> Purge well therein, for it is good
> To help thy body and cleanse thy blood.
> Neve's *Almanack* 1633

'A purging ale, to be taken in April. Take the strongest ale you can get, and leave in it a bag with crushed senna, polypody of the oak, bay-berries, ash-keys, aniseeds and fennel seeds: drink thereof about a pint morning and evening, it purgeth the body mightily.'
Mrs Harrington's Book, 18th century

'On the Feast of St Urban (forsooth) maids hang up some of their hair before the image of St Urban, because they would have the rest of their hair grow long and golden.'
Reginald Scot *The Discovery of Witchcraft* 1584

3 Easter falls during April in most years.

Easter commemorates the Resurrection of Christ, which took place at the Jewish Passover or 'Pesach', whence Easter is called *Pascha* in Latin. Since the Passover is a 'movable' festival, connected with the first full moon of spring, the date of Easter also varies considerably.

'Easter-day' (says the *Book of Common Prayer*) 'is always the first Sunday after the first Full Moon which happens next after the One and twentieth day of March' (the Spring Equinox), 'and if the Full Moon happens upon a Sunday, Easter-day is the Sunday after.' Thus Easter may fall upon any of the thirty-five days between March the Twenty-second and April the Twenty-fifth, both inclusive.

The English name of Easter, ironically, perpetuates a pagan rather than a biblical festival of spring rebirth: that of the Anglo-Saxon dawn goddess Eostra. Her sacred animal was apparently a hare, just possibly the ancestor of the 'Easter bunny'.

4 Beware Springtime agues, and other excesses.

'Dr Butler lying at the Savoy in London, next the water side, where there was a Balcony looked into the Thames, a Patient came to him that was grievously tormented with an Ague. The Doctor orders a boat to be in readiness under the window, and discoursed with the patient on the Balcony: when, on a signal given, two or three lusty Fellows came behind the Gentleman and threw him a matter of twenty feet into the Thames. This surprise absolutely cured him.'

John Aubrey *Brief Lives* late 17th century

'Beware of venerious acts before the first sleep, and especially beware of such things after dinner or after a full stomach: for it doth engender the cramp, the gout, the ague and other displeasures.'

Andrew Boorde *Dietary of Health* 1547

Passion Sunday – the fifth in Lent – falls in early April when Easter is late: make Passion Dock (or Bistort) Puddings.

5

The many-named Bistort – or 'twice-twisted' because of its contorted snake-like root, whence it is also known as Adderwort – is called Passion Dock or Easter Ledgers in northern England: and there (especially in Cumbria) Bistort puddings are eaten during the Passiontide weeks before Easter.

To make Easter Ledge pudding. Take a pound each of young Passion Docks and young nettles and a large onion, and chop them small: then put to them a tea-cup full of washed barley and half a teaspoon of salt and mix them together. Boil them in a muslin bag for two hours, and then beat them with an egg, butter, salt and pepper, and oatmeal if you wish. Eat the pudding fried with eggs and bacon or veal.

Lady Day, Old Style: Alexander the Great's birthday: swallows begin to appear.

6

> On Lady Day the later
> The cold goes o'er the water.

The weather generally shows a marked improvement at about this time.

'Upon April the sixth, Alexander the Great was born. Upon the same day he conquered Darius, won a great Victory at sea, and died the same day.'
John Aubrey *Miscellanies* 1695

'In whatsoever house the swallow breedeth, the goodman of the house is not there made cuckold, what day soever he be married on.'
Gerard Legh *Accedence of Armory* 1562

7 Hedgehogs again active after winter hibernation.

'The hedgehog's meat is apples, worms and grapes: when he findeth them upon the earth, he rolleth on them until he hath filled up all his prickles, and then carrieth them home to his den . . . and so forth he goeth, making a noise like a cart wheel. The prickly thorns on their backs will not suffer them to have copulation like Dogs or Swine, and for this cause they are a very little while in copulation, because they cannot stand long belly to belly upon their hind legs. With the same skin flayed off, and the prickles, brushes are made for garments, so that they complain ill which affirm that there is no good nor profit from this beast.'
Edward Topsell *History of Four-footed Beasts* 1607

'For a lunatic. Take a hedge-hog and make broth of him, and let the patient eat of the broth and flesh.'
Fairfax Household Book, 17th/18th century

8 Collect Easter eggs – otherwise Pasch, Pace or Peace Eggs – for Easter feasts and games.

Herrings, herrings white and red
Ten a penny, Lent's dead
Rise Dame and give a Negg
Or else a piece of bacon
One for Peter, two for Paul
Three for Jack-a-Lents all
Away, Lent, away.
Oxfordshire children's rhyme, from John Aubrey's
Remains of Gentilism 1688

To name and dye Pace Eggs. First hard-boil them in plain water, and while they are still warm write your name on them with a sharpened candle-end. Then boil them again with gorse-blossom for a yellow colour, cochineal for red, onion-skins or nettle-roots for yellow-green or Pasque flowers for bright green. The dye will not take on the candle-wax, so your name will stand out in white.

Early new potatoes now ready.

9

>   Plant your taters when you will
>   They won't come up until April.

'The prepared roots of Potatoes of Virginia stop fluxes of the Bowels, nourish much, and restore Pining Consumptions: being boiled, baked, or roasted, they are eaten with Butter, Salt, Juice of Lemons and double refined Sugar, as common food: and they increase seed and provoke Lust, causing Fruitfullness in both sexes.'
>   William Salmon *Herbal* 1710

'The use of these potatoes was forbidden in Burgundy (where they call them Indian artichokes) for that they were persuaded the too frequent use of them caused the Leprosy.'
>   Gerard *Herbal* 1597

'The man that hath not anything to boast but his illustrious ancestors is like a potato: the only good belonging to him is underground.'
>   Thomas Overbury *Characters* 1637

Open beehives: and candy Spring flowers.

10

'In April open the doors of Bee-hives, for now they hatch, that they may reap the benefit of Flowery Spring: and be careful of your Bees.'
>   Worlidge *Systema Agriculturae* 1697

'To Candy all kind of Flowers as they grow, with their stalks on. Take the Flowers and cut the stalk somewhat short: then take one pound of the whitest and hardest Sugar, put to it eight spoons of Rosewater, and boil it till it will roll between your finger and your thumb. Then take it from the fire, and as it waxeth cold dip in all your Flowers: and taking them out suddenly, lay them one by one in the bottom of a sieve. Then turn a stool with the feet upwards, set the sieve on the feet, cover it with a fair linen cloth, and set a chafing-dish of coals in the midst of the stool underneath the sieve: the heat thereof will dry your Candy presently. Then box them up, and they will keep all the year, and look very pleasantly.'
>   Thomas Jenner *A Book of Fruits and Flowers* 1653

11

Many trees now coming into leaf: prognosticate a wet or a dry summer from the budding of oak and ash.

> Oak before Ash
> We'll only have a splash
> Ash before Oak
> We're in for a soak.

'For a stinking breath, take Oak buds when they are new budded out and distill them, then let the party grieved nine mornings and nine evenings drink of it; then forbear a while, and take it again.'
Markham *The English Housewife* 1683

> Avoid the oak
> It courts the stroke
> And shun the ash
> It courts the flash.

Do not, therefore, stand under oak or ash trees during a thunderstorm.

12

Reprove springtime indiscretions: but discreetly.

'If you have a dear female friend, whom you suspect of any youthful excursions, especially levity, and would reduce her to a better understanding, mildly lay open her errors; and therein discover what an enemy she hath been to God and her own reputation. But that she may not think your reproofs have their original from malice or hatred to her person, declare what a great esteem you ever had for her excellent parts and rare endowments of mind: and what a pity it is, such excellencies should be eclipsed by such foul miscarriages.'
Hannah Woolley *The Gentlewoman's Companion* 1675

'For the green-sickness, or for a love-sick maid. Take earth-worms, open them, wash them clean, dry them in an oven and beat them to powder. Give thereof two spoonfulls in white wine in the morning.'
Fairfax Household Book, 17th/18th century

An April Fish
Is a dainty dish.

13

'There is not any Exercise more pleasing nor agreeable to a truly sober and ingenious man, than this of Angling. It wearieth not a man over-much: it injureth no man, so that it be in an open large water: he being esteemed a Beast rather than a Man that will oppose this Exercise: neither doth it in any wise debauch him that useth it. The delight of it also, rouses up the Ingenious early in the Spring-mornings, that they have the benefit of the sweet and pleasant Morning air, which many through sluggishness enjoy not.'

Worlidge *Systema Agriculturae* 1697

First cuckoos heard about now: be sure to react promptly and properly when you hear them.

14

The cuckoo is a merry bird, she sings as she flies
She brings us good tidings, she tells us no lies
She dries up the dirt in the Spring of the year
And sucks little birds eggs to keep her voice clear.

Sussex rhyme

Gang and hear the gowk yell
Sit and see the swallow flee
'Twill be a happy year with thee.

It is lucky to be walking when you hear the first cuckoo – or 'gowk' in Scots – and to be sitting when you see the first swallow: but if you hear the first cuckoo from your bed, you or someone in your family will die that year. If you have no money in your pocket when she calls, or if you fail to turn over all the coins you have, you will be poor all the year: but if you immediately sit down and take off your left shoe, you will find in it a hair of exactly the same colour as that of your true love.

'If, when you first hear the cuckoo, you mark well where your right foot standeth, and take up of that earth, the fleas will by no means breed where any of that same earth is scattered.'

Thomas Hill *Natural and Artificial Conclusions* 1650

15

The innocent Cuckoo Flower – or Ladysmock, or Milkmaids – and the blatant Cuckoo Pint now blooming.

Because of its rod-in-sheath flower, the Cuckoo Pint – originally Cuckoo Pintle, or cuckoo's penis – has many local names like Dog Cocks, Lords and Ladies, Priest's Pintle, Stallions and Mares and Wake Robin. Its corrosive root, moreover, could be made into a dangerous aphrodisiac – and could be used, with care, for other purposes.

'The fresh roots, cut small, will make excellent sport with a saucy sharking guest, and drive him from overmuch boldness, strewed upon any dainty bit that is given him to eat . . . for within a while after taking it, it will so burn and prick his mouth that he shall not be able to eat any more, or scarce speak for pain.'

William Coles *Adam in Eden* 1657

16

Maundy Thursday falls about now when Easter is late.

At the Last Supper on the night before His crucifixion on Good Friday, Christ symbolically washed the feet of His disciples: and gave them 'a new commandment. . . that ye love one another, as I have loved you'. This commandment – in Latin *mandatum*, whence 'Maundy' – gives the Thursday before Good Friday its name: and on that day kings, bishops and other great personages traditionally washed the feet of as many paupers as they had years of age.

Thus, in 1572, Queen Elizabeth I 'kneeling down upon the cushions and carpets under the feet of the poor women, first washed one foot of every one of them in so many several basins of warm water and sweet flowers . . . then wiped, crossed and kissed them, as the almoner and others had done before'. It should be emphasized that the paupers' feet had already been cleansed three times (by a laundress, the sub-almoner and the almoner) before Her Majesty touched them.

**Good Friday comes this month, the old woman
runs
With one-a-penny, two-a-penny, Hot Cross
Buns
Whose virtue is, if you'll believe what's said
They'll not grow mouldy like common bread.**

Poor Robin's Almanack 1733

In memory of the kindly woman who, it is said, offered Christ a loaf on His way to Calvary, no bread or buns baked on Good Friday will ever grow mouldy: and a piece of dried Good Friday loaf grated into milk is sure to cure all stomach ailments. Hot cross buns also protect sailors from shipwreck, and houses from fire: but only if they are baked on Good Friday itself.

Because a mocking washerwoman allegedly threw dirty water at Christ on the first Good Friday, however, to wash clothes then will bring death to the family: and clothes hung out to dry will be spotted with blood.

Most forms of work, indeed, will prove unlucky on this most solemn and ill-omened of days: and it is especially dangerous to use any iron tools or to drive any nails, lest you crucify Christ anew.

Good Friday, nevertheless, is thought the best possible time to plant potatoes, beans, peas and parsley – though it is safest to use a wooden spade for the purpose. Buried like Christ today, the crops will spring up and flourish like Him soon afterwards.

Make Eastertide Tansies.

'To make a Tansy. Take three pints of Cream, fourteen New-laid eggs (the whites of seven put away) one pint of juice of Spinnach, six or seven spoonfuls of juice of Tansy, a Nutmeg (or two) grated small, half a pound of sugar, and a little salt. Beat all these well together, then fry it in a pan with no more Butter than is necessary. When it is enough, serve it up with juice of Orange or slices of Lemon upon it.'

The Closet of Sir Kenelm Digby Opened 1669

19

On Easter Sunday morning the rising sun dances for joy at the Resurrection, and it is best seen to do so from hilltops. Yet the Devil often puts clouds in the way, or dims the sight of those who look straight at the sun: so look at its reflection in a stream or a bowl of water, and you will certainly see it dance.

> At Easter let your clothes be new
> Or else be sure you will it rue.

If you do not wear some article of completely new clothing on Easter Day, you will be unlucky all the year: and at the very least 'the birds will make a mess on you'. New Easter bonnets are particularly popular, but any new clothes worn for the first time to church on Easter Sunday will thereafter bring you good fortune whenever you put them on. At any time of the year, indeed, new clothes should be worn to church before they are worn anywhere else.

20

On Easter Monday and Tuesday – or on the second Monday and Tuesday after Easter – bands of 'lifters' or 'heavers' roamed the towns of north-western England and the Welsh Borders, intent on carrying out a custom which was supposed to represent the 'raising up' – or Resurrection – of Christ.

'On the first day, a party of men go with a chair into every house to which they can get admission, force every female to be seated in their vehicle, and lift them three times with loud huzzas: for this they claim the reward of a chaste salute, which those who are too coy to submit to may get an exemption from by a fine of one shilling. On the Tuesday the women claim the same privilege, and pursue their business in the same manner.'   *The Public Advertiser* 1787

'Not bearing in mind the season of the year, he ventured on a short cut. Until half-way through there was no sign of danger, but when fairly in the net, out bounced a bevy of beautiful nymphs who barred further passage, and one of the most stalwart seized and fairly heaved him off the ground, claiming and receiving the silver guerdon demanded as the forfeit.'
Letter from Wolverhampton, 1838

The Sun enters the House of Taurus.

21

'He that is born under Taurus shall be strong, hardy, and full of strife. In his youth he will despise every person and be ireful: he shall go on pilgrimage and live among strangers. He shall be rich by women, and yet shall experience many pains by women. He shall be grieved by sickness and venom at twenty-three, and in peril of water at thirty-three: and shall live eighty-five years and three months.

'The woman shall be effectual, labouring, and a great liar. She shall have many husbands and many children. She shall be at her best estate at sixteen years: but then sickly, and if she escape shall live seventy-five years. She ought to bear rings and precious stones about her.

'As well man as woman shall be likened to the bull that laboureth the land: but when the seed is sown, he hath but the straw to his part. They shall keep well their own, and be reputed unkind.'

Kalendar of Shepheardes 1604

Make prognostications from the neck and throat, which are governed by Taurus, and seek cures for them.

22

'The neck short, signifieth one to be witty: such as are strong about the knot or joint of the neck are of good capacity; such as are weak, are dullards. The neck big, to be strong; big and fleshy, to be ireful; the neck long and small, signifieth to be fearful.'

The Shepherd's Prognostication 1729

'For a Sore Throat the best medicine. Take quince seeds and steep them in rose water two hours at least, the longer the better. Then take the rose water and gargle in your mouth: this do till the throat is well, it will cure it in a few times taking.'

Robert Cook's Receipt Book, *c.* 1730

'If a pin, a thorn or fishbone stick in one's mouth, let him rub the outside against it with a little cat's dung, and it will easily come forth.'

Edward Topsell *History of Four-footed Beasts* 1607

23 St George's Day: beware of dragons.

To save a Maid, St George the Dragon slew
A pretty tale, if all is told be true
Most say, there are no Dragons, and tis said
There was no George: pray God there was a Maid.
John Aubrey *Remains of Gentilism* 1688

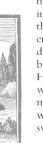

'This serpent (or dragon as some call it) is reputed to be nine feet, or rather more, in length, and shaped almost in the form of an axletree of a cart: a quantity of thickness in the middest, and somewhat smaller at both ends. . . . There are likewise upon either side of him discovered, two great bunches so big as a large football, and (as some think) will in time grow to wings. . . . He will cast his venom about four rods from him, as by woeful experience it was proved on the bodies of a man and woman coming that way, who were afterwards found dead, being poisoned and very much swelled.'

A True and Wonderful Discourse
relating a strange and monstrous Serpent
lately discovered . . . in Sussex, 1614

24 St Mark's Eve: try the church-porch watch – if you dare.

If you wish to know which of your neighbours are to die in the coming year, go to the church porch at eleven o'clock on St Mark's Eve night and remain there for two hours. During that time the phantoms of the doomed will be seen passing into the church, and some say that they will appear as at the moment of death, the suicides with a rope about their neck and the drowned as if floundering in water. Some report, too, that the spirits of those who will recover from dangerous illnesses also enter, but are later seen to return: and that the likenesses of those to be married enter and exit in couples. You may need to repeat the process in three successive years before any spirits appear: but beware, for if you see your own double – or fall asleep while the ghostly procession passes – you will surely die within the twelvemonth; and if you try the church-porch watch but once, you may be compelled to repeat it every year until you 'meet yourself'.

APRIL

St Mark's Day: cowslips now blooming.

 25

Despite their name (a polite form of 'cow-slops' or cow-pats, from which they were believed to be engendered), cowslips have long been used as an aid to beauty.

'An ointment being made of cowslips takes away spots and wrinkles of the skin, sun-burning, and freckles, and adds beauty exceedingly.'

Culpeper *Herbal* 1653

'The flowers of cowslips conserved in sugar and also the stilled water thereof are very good for them that are weak and very low brought by long sickness, and it hath a singular property to comfort the heart.'

William Turner *Herbal* 1568

'Three or four handfuls of cowslip-flowers, cast into a bath very hot, take away tiredness.'

Mrs Harrington's Book, 18th century

On this day, according to tradition, 'The Waters of the Flood began to abate, and the Ark rested'.

 26

'When thou seest in the Morning a Rainbow, it betokeneth Rain, and a great boisterous Storm; when it doth appear at three or four in the Afternoon, it betokeneth fair weather and a strong dew; when at the going down of the Sun, then doth it for the most part Thunder and Rain. When it appeareth in the East, then followeth fair weather, or when in the North, fair weather and clear.'

The Shepherd's Prognostication 1729

Rainbow to windward, foul falls the day
Rainbow to leeward, rain runs away.

When you see a rainbow, bow to it, for it is God's token of peace between Him and mankind: but to point at it is very unlucky.

27

Marriage, frowned on in Lent, is once again permitted from the Sunday after Easter: and since May marriages are unlucky, take the opportunity to wed during these last days of April.

'There was formerly a custom in the North of England, which will be thought to have bordered very closely upon Indecency, and strongly marks the Grossness of Manners that prevailed among our Ancestors. It was for the young men present at a Wedding to strive immediately after the Ceremony, who could first pluck off the Bride's Garters from her legs. This was done before the very Altar. Whoever were so fortunate as to be Victors in this singular species of Contest (during which the Bride was often obliged to scream out, and was very frequently thrown down) bore the Garter about the Church in triumph.'

Brand *Observations of Popular Antiquities* 1813

28

With uncanny May Eve approaching, be sure to guard your children against witches.

'He (the Devil) teacheth witches to make ointments of the bowels and members of children, whereby they ride in the air, and accomplish all their desires. So as, if there be any children unbaptized, or not guarded with the sign of the cross or orisons: then the witches may and do catch them from their mother's sides at night, or out of their cradles . . . and after burial steal them out of graves, and seethe them in a cauldron, until their flesh be made potable.'

Reginald Scot *The Discovery of Witchcraft* 1584

A crust of salted bread under the baby's pillow will keep off witches, but to be sure, hang garlic and rowan-leaves round the cradle as well, and leave a bible among the bedclothes. Though efficacious against baby-stealers, a knife jammed point upwards near the cradle is perhaps not to be recommended for babies: and the very best way to protect them is to have them christened as soon as possible.

Put Taurean bulls to cows now for early calves next year.

29

'Every Bull is sufficient for ten cows, and the Bulls must not feed with cows, for two months before their leaping time, and then let them come together without restraint. If the Bull then be slow and heavy, take the tail of an Hart and burn it to powder, then moisten it in wine and rub therewith the genitals of the Bull, and he will rise above measure into Lust – wherefore, if it be more than tolerable, it must be allayed with oil. They are a great while in copulation, and some have guessed by certain signs, whether the calf will prove male or female: for, say they, if the Bull leap down on the right side of the Cow, it will be a male, if on the left a female. If a man then desire a male calf, let him tie up the right stone of the Bull at the time of copulation: and for a female, bind up the left.'

Edward Topsell *History of Four-footed Beasts* 1607

May Eve: the Eve of Beltane ('bright-fire'), the Celtic festival of Summer's beginning.

30

To make the Beltane fire in the Welsh manner. First be sure that none of the company have any iron or metal about them, neither coins, knives or buttons. Then let nine men gather nine types of wood, and lay the sticks crosswise within a circle marked on the earth: the fire is best made on a hilltop, and all other fires within sight of it must be extinguished. The Beltane fire must then be kindled by rubbing oak-twigs together, and on no account with matches or any artificial aids.

Evil spirits are not the only dangers facing those who dare to go a-Maying tonight.

'I have heard it credibly reported by men of great gravity, credit and reputation; that of forty, threescore or a hundred maids going to the wood over night, there have scarcely the third part of them returned home again undefiled.'

Philip Stubbes *The Anatomy of Abuses* 1586

MAY

Milk and May-games

Probably named after Maia, a Roman goddess of growth and increase.

In Welsh: *Mai*

In Gaelic: *Mios bochuin* – the month of swelling.

In Anglo-Saxon: *Thrimilci* – the month when cows give milk thrice a day; the dairy month.

MAY

May Day: Beltane, the Celtic festival of Summer's beginning.

'May' – which should be gathered at or before sunrise – can be any kind of flowering greenery, though hawthorn (or 'May-blossom'), birch, and rowan are the favourites, while sloe or blackthorn is ill-omened. To leave a branch of hawthorn at a friend's door is a luck-bringing compliment: but 'gifts' of other kinds of tree can be insulting.

> Nut for a slut; plum for the glum
> Bramble if she ramble; gorse for the whores.

> A fair maid who, the first of May
> Goes to the fields at break of day
> And washes in dew from the hawthorn tree
> Will ever after handsome be.

Some say the best May-dew is found beneath oaks, or on ivy leaves: and you should make a secret wish as you wash your face in it.

'But the chiefest jewel they bring from thence is their May pole, which they bring home with great veneration. . . . This May pole (this stinking Idol rather) is covered all over with flowers and herbs, bound round about with strings from the top to the bottom, and sometimes painted with variable colours. . . . Then fall they to leap and dance about it, as the Heathen people did at the dedication of their idols, whereof this is the perfect pattern, or rather the thing itself.'
Philip Stubbes *The Anatomy of Abuses* 1583

Cows now coming into full milk for May dairying.

'The Cow chose for the Dairy must have all the signs of plenty of Milk: as a crumpled Horn, thin Neck, a hairy dew-lap, and a very large Udder, with Teats long, thick and sharp at the ends: the Udder to be either all white (of what colour soever the Cow be) or at least the fore part thereof.'
Markham *The English Housewife* 1683

'Cow's milk is not good for them which have gurgulations in the belly, but it is very good for melancholy men, and for old men and children.'
Andrew Boorde *Dietary of Health* 1547

3

The Feast of the Finding of the Holy Cross, alias Cross-mass or Rood Day: 'Avoiding Day' in Scotland.

In England, Cross-mass was a fortunate day for putting bulls to cows: but in Scotland it is most ill-omened, because it is also the 'Avoiding Day' when the evil angels were cast out (or 'avoided') from Heaven. These supernatural nuisances sulkily haunt the earth on the anniversary of their downfall, and make it a very unlucky day to start a journey or begin a task, to marry or to count livestock.

> Sweep with a broom that is cut in May
> You'll sweep the head of the house away.

It is unlucky to buy, or use, any new broom or brush during this month.

4

Be careful of your health and diet, and eat sage this month.

'In May be no sluggard, for the bed is unwholesome. Clarified whey this month is a most sovereign drink, and sage is an excellent breakfast. Young lettuce is an approved salad, but the entrails or offal of beasts should by all means be refused: neither go wetshod in the dew in the morning.'

Drake's *Almanack* 1639

'The eating of Sage in the month of May, with Butter, Parsley and some Salt is very commendable to the Body: as also Sage-ale made with it is good for Teeming women, such as are subject to miscarry through the too much moisture or slipperyness of their Wombs. At all times be sure you wash your Sage, for fear that Toads (who as I conceive come to to relieve themselves being overcharged with poison) should leave some of the Venom on the leaves, the danger whereof is on record: therefore it is good to plant Rue among your Sage, and then they will not come near it.'

William Coles *Adam in Eden* 1657

Take heed to thy Bees, that are ready to swarm
The loss thereof now, is a crown's worth of harm.

Tusser *Five Hundred Points of Good Husbandry* 1573

If bees 'swarm' and leave their hives to establish new colonies during May, they will produce good honey that year. When they do so, you are entitled by custom to follow them over anyone's land and claim them when they come to rest: but only so long as you 'ting-tang' as you go, by beating on some metal utensil – the sound whereof is also said to make your bees stop.

'Their hours of swarming are for the most part between the hours of ten and three, and they ought to be watched every day.'

Hillman *Tusser Redivivus* 1710

A swarm in May
Is worth a load of hay
A swarm in June
Is worth a silver spoon
A swarm in July
Is not worth a fly

Observe the weather: May herb salads now in season.

Button to chin, till May be in
Cast not a clout, till May be out.

Some say the second line means you must not shed clothing until June; others that it is safe to do so when 'May' (or hawthorn) blooms – which even then is sometimes not until well into May.

'To make a Sallet of all kinds of Herbs. Take your Herbs (as the tops of red Sage, Mint, Lettuce, Violets, Marigold, Spinach etcetera) and pick them very fine in fair water: and wash your flowers by themselves, and swing them in a strainer. Then mingle them in a dish with Cucumbers and Lemons pared and sliced: scrape thereon Sugar and put in Vinegar and Oil. Spread your Flowers on top of the Sallet, and take Eggs boiled hard and lay them about the Dish.'

Thomas Jenner *A Book of Fruits and Flowers* 1653

7
The white-flowered, sour-apple tasting Wood Sorrel now in bloom: children born this week have special powers.

'Wood Sorrel or Cuckoo Sorrel: the Apothecaries and Herbalists call it Alleluya, and Panis Cuculi, or Cuckoo's Meat, because either the Cuckoo feedeth thereon or by reason when it springeth forth and flowereth the Cuckoo singeth most, at which time also Alleluya was wont to be sung in churches. Stamped and used for green sauce, it is good for them that have sick and feeble stomachs: for it strengtheneth the stomach, procureth appetite: and of all Sorrel sauces is the best, not only in virtue, but also in the pleasantness of the taste.'

Gerard *Herbal* 1633

Children 'born between the Beltanes' – between the first and the eighth of May, the beginning and end of the Beltane festival – have 'the skill of man and beast', and power over both.

8
'Furry Day' or Floral Dance Day at Helston in Cornwall: Robin Hood May Games in full swing.

'I came once myself to a place, riding a journey homeward from London, and sent word overnight to the town that I would preach there in the morning, because it was an Holy-day. I thought I should have found a great company in the church; but when I came there, the church door was fast locked. I tarried there half an hour and more; at last the key was found, and one of the parish comes to me and says: "This is a busy day with us, we cannot hear you; this is Robin Hood's day, the parish is gone abroad to gather for Robin Hood." I thought my bishop's rochet should have been regarded, though I were not: but it would not serve, and I was fain to give place to Robin Hood's men.'

Bishop Latimer *Sixth Sermon before Edward VI* 1549

Milk your cows carefully.

9

'The woman must sit on the near side of the Cow, and she must gently at the first handle and stretch her Dugs, and moisten them with Milk, that they may yield out the Milk the better, and with less pain. She shall not settle herself to milk, nor fix her Pail firm to the ground, till she see the Cow stand sure and firm, but be ready upon any motion of the Cow to save her Pail from overturning. She shall then milk the cow boldly, and not leave stretching or straining of her teats, till not one drop of Milk more will come from them: for the worst point of Housewifery that can be is to leave a Cow half milked . . . it is the only way to make a Cow dry, and utterly unprofitable for the Dairy. She shall do nothing rashly or suddenly about the Cow, which may frighten or amaze her; but as she came gently, so with all gentleness she shall depart.'

Markham *The English Housewife* 1683

'Dotterel Day': the high point of the bird–netting season.

10

'The dotterel is a very foolish bird, but excellent meat, and with us accounted a great delicacy. It is taken in the night time by the light of candle, by imitating the gestures of the fowler: for if he stretches out an arm, that also stretches out of a wing; if he a foot, that likewise a foot; in brief, whatever the fowler doth, the same doth the bird; and so being intent upon men's gestures, it is deceived and covered with the net spread for it.'

Willoughby *Ornithology* 1678

'All manner of small birds be good and light of digestion, except sparrows, which be hard of digestion. Titmouses, colemouses and wrens, the which eat spiders and poisons, be not commendable: of all small birds the lark is best, then is praised the blackbird and thrush.'

Andrew Boorde *Dietary of Health* 1547

11 Ascension Day and Rogationtide are nearly always celebrated during May.

Forty days after His Resurrection, Christ was taken up to Heaven on Ascension Day, or Holy Thursday, which is therefore a movable feast, falling forty days after Easter. The three days preceding it, when priests and people traditionally processed the fields chanting prayers ('rogations') for God's blessing on the growing crops, are called 'Rogationtide', and are also the favourite season for 'Beating the Bounds' of parishes. During these processions, local boys were customarily 'remembered' of parish boundary markers by being beaten over them, until milder convention decreed that markers rather than boys should be beaten. For adults, however, 'Rogation gangings' were festive events, enlivened by much 'perambulation beer' and picnic feasting.

'I will not speak of the rage and furor of these uplandish processions and gangings about, which be spent in rioting and beastly belly-cheer.'

Banks *Epistles and Gospels*

12 St Pancras's Day: seek headache cures: Lady's Mantle in flower.

St Pancras, a Roman boy martyred at the age of fourteen, is one of the patrons of children, and is invoked against headaches.

'To make a Worm come out of the head. Take in May the marrow of a bull or cow and put it warm into the ear, and the worm will come forth for sweetness of the marrow.'

Fairfax Household Book, 17th/18th century

'Our Lady's Mantle is an herb of green colour and groweth in moist meadows. In the night it closeth itself together like a purse, and in the morning it is found full of dew.'

William Turner *Herbal* 1568

'The Decoction of Lady's Mantle drunk, and the bruised herb outwardly applied, helpeth to keep down maiden's Paps or Dugs: as also to bring back the Breasts of Women that are too big, or over-sagging to their due bigness and hardness.'

William Coles *Adam in Eden* 1657

MAY

May Day, Old Style: morris dancers much in request for May Games and Whitsun Feasts.

13

'They tie about either leg twenty or forty bells, with rich handkerchiefs in their hands . . . borrowed for the most part of their pretty Mopsies and loving Besses, for bussing them in the dark. . . . Then march this heathen company towards the Church and Churchyard, their pipers piping, their drummers thundering, their stumps dancing, their bells jangling, their handkerchiefs swinging about their heads like madmen, their hobby horses and other monsters skirmishing amongst the rout. And in this sort they go to the Church, and into the Church (though the Minister be at prayer or preaching) dancing and swinging their handkerchiefs over their heads like devils incarnate, with such a confused noise, that no man can hear his own voice.'
Philip Stubbes *The Anatomy of Abuses* 1583

'We never read of any Christians that went dancing into Heaven. . . . The gate of Heaven is too strait, the way to bliss too narrow, for whole Troops of Dancers to march in together. Men never yet went to Heaven by multitudes, much less by Morris-Dancing troops.'
William Prynne *Histriomastix* 1632

Beware the effects of vaccination.

14

On this day in 1796, Edward Jenner first inoculated against smallpox by infecting a boy with immunizing cowpox germs, taken from a milkmaid's hand. His opponents, however, spread the tale that those vaccinated would turn into cows, like 'a child at Peckham who, after being inoculated with the cow pox, had his former natural disposition absolutely changed; so that it ran upon all fours bellowing like a cow, and butting with its head like a bull.'

15

This month is the best of all for butter-making.

'There be many mischiefs and inconveniences which may happen to butter in the churning, because it is a body of much tenderness, and neither will endure much heat nor much cold: for if it be overheated, it will look white, crumble, and be bitter in taste; and if it be over-cold it will not come at all, but will make you waste much labour in vain.'

Markham *The English Housewife* 1683

A charm to make butter come: repeat it three times.

> Come butter come
> Come butter come
> Peter stands at the gate
> Waiting for a buttered cake
> Come butter come.

Ady *A Candle in the Dark* 1655

16

Changelings often substituted for mortal children during May.

'The complexion of this supposed Changeling was perfectly delicate . . . he never spoke nor cried . . . and was very seldom seen to smile: but if anyone called him a Fairy-Elf he would frown, and fix his eyes earnestly on those who said it, as though he would look them through. . . . The neighbours have often looked in at the window to see how he behaved when alone . . . and were sure to find him laughing, and in the utmost delight. This made them judge that he was not without Company more pleasing to him than any mortal's could be; and what made this conjecture seem the more reasonable was, that if he were left never so dirty, the woman at her return found him with a clean face and his hair combed with the utmost exactness.'

Waldron *Description of the Isle of Man* 1731

'This day sessions ended at the Old Bailey, where three received Sentence of Death for Extorting Money from Persons, by threatening to accuse them of Sodomy: which the Court observed was equal to Robbery on the Highway.'

St James's Evening Post May the 16th 1719

MAY

Comfrey, that invaluable herb, now coming into flower: shun excessive pill-taking.

17

'Comfrey is a very common but a very neglected plant: it contains very great virtues. Yea, it is said to be so powerful to consolidate and knit together, that if it be boiled with dissevered pieces of flesh in a pot, it will join them together again.'

Culpeper *Herbal* 1653

'The slimy substance of the root made in a posset of ale, and given to drink against the pain in the back, gotten by any violent motion (as wrestling, or the overmuch use of women) doth in four or five days perfectly cure the same, although the involuntary flowing of the seed in men be gotten thereby.'

Gerard *Herbal* 1633

On this day in 1817 died Mr Samuel Jessup of Heckington in Lincolnshire, a bachelor 'who possessed a most inordinate craving for physic': during the last twenty-one years of his life he swallowed at least 226,934 pills (51,590 of them in 1814 alone). 'Notwithstanding this, and the addition of 40,000 bottles of mixture, juleps and electuaries . . . the deceased lived to attain the advanced age of 65 years.'

Hone *Every-Day Book* 1829

Kittens born in May grow into unlucky, melancholy cats.

18

Though cat (a good mouser) doth dwell in a house
Yet ever in dairy have trap for a mouse.

Tusser *Five Hundred Points of Good Husbandry* 1573

'There is in some men a natural dislike and abhorring of cats; their natures being so composed, that not only when they see them, but being near them and unseen (and hid of purpose) such men fall into passions, frettings and sweatings, pulling off their hats and trembling fearfully.'

Edward Topsell *History of Four-footed Beasts* 1607

MAY

19

Water which falls at Ascensiontide – forty days after Easter – is holy: well-dressing now in season.

Because the skies were opened to receive Christ on Ascension Day, any rain which falls then comes straight from Heaven: so it has special curative properties, being particularly good for bathing sore eyes. Water from holy wells is also uniquely efficacious if collected early on 'Holy Thursday' morning: and Ascensiontide or Whitsun are the favourite seasons for 'well-dressing'.

'One year in the Presbyterian times in the Civil Wars they neglected the anniversary Dressing of the Salt-well at Droitwich: and afterward the Spring became dry, to the great loss of the Town. So afterwards they revived their annual custom (notwithstanding the power of the Parliament), and ever since, volens nolens the Minister there (and also the Soldiers) they did and will Dress it, and the salt-water returned again and still continues.'

John Aubrey *Remains of Gentilism* 1688

20

To marry in May is notoriously unlucky, and to do so in an ill-omened green dress is sheer madness.

Married in May and kirked in green
Both bride and bridegroom won't long be seen.

O' marriages in May
Bairns die in decay.

'On May the twentieth 1736 the corpse of Samuel Baldwin was immersed in the sea off the Needles, on the Hampshire coast. This was performed in consequence of an earnest wish the deceased had expressed, in order to disappoint the intention of his wife: she had repeatedly assured him in their domestic squabbles (which were very frequent) that if she survived him she would revenge her conjugal sufferings by dancing on his grave.'

Hone *Year Book* 1826

In these 'Frankin's Days', beware late and destructive frosts, thunder and unreliable weather.

21

According to a Devon legend, the sharp frosts which sometimes occur at about this time are the revenge of one Frankin, a beer-brewer put out of business by competition from cider. He therefore vowed his soul to the Devil in return for frosts on each of the three 'Frankin's Days' around May the twenty-first, hoping that these would kill the apple-blossom and ruin the cider crop.

> Shear your sheep in May
> You'll shear them all away.

May weather is considered too unreliable for shorn sheep, which may take cold and die: and thunder this month presages a poor summer and a bad harvest.

> Thunder in May
> Frightens the Summer away.

The Sun enters the House of Gemini.

22

'The man born under Gemini shall have many wounds. He shall lead an open and reasonable life, he shall receive much money, he will go in unknown places, and he will not bide in the place of his Nativity. His first wife shall not live long, but he shall marry strange women. He shall be bitten of a dog, he shall have a mark of iron or fire. He shall pass the sea, and live an hundred years and ten months.

'The woman shall come to honour: but she shall be aggrieved of a false crime. She ought to be wedded at fourteen years, if she shall be chaste and endure all peril: she shall live seventy years and honour God.

'As well man as woman shall augment and assemble goods for their successors: but scantly shall they use their own goods, they shall be so avaricious.'

The Kalendar of Shepheardes 1604

23

Make prognostications from the hands, which are ruled by Gemini.

'A long hand and long fingers, betoken a man not only apt for mechanical artifice, but liberally ingenious: but those short note a fool and fit for nothing. An hard brawny hand signs dull and rude; a soft hand, witty but effeminate; an hairy hand, luxurious. The often clapping and folding of the hands, notes covetousness; and an ambidexter is noted for ireful, crafty and injurious. If his fingers crook upwards, that shows him liberal; if downward, niggardly.'

Gaule *Mag-astro-Mancer Posed and Puzzled* 1652

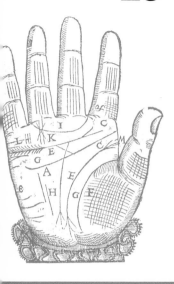

'I have seen some Rings made for Sweet-hearts with a Heart enamelled between two right hands . . . two Rings were made by Queen Elizabeth's appointment, which being laid one upon another showed the like figure. The Heart was two Diamonds, which being joined made the Heart. Queen Elizabeth kept one moiety and sent the other as a token of her constant Friendship to Mary Queen of Scots: but she cut off her Head for all that.'

John Aubrey *Remains of Gentilism* 1688

24

Whitsun, or Pentecost (Greek *pentikosti* – 'fiftieth day') is a movable feast, falling fifty days after Easter. It commemorates the descent of the Holy Spirit, in the form of tongues of fire, upon the assembled Disciples: and because of the understanding (or 'wit') thus bestowed on them, the festival's English name is sometimes glossed as 'Wit Sunday'. Originally, however, it was 'White Sunday', from the white 'robes of innocence' worn by the converts traditionally baptized at this season.

'Against Whit Sunday or some other time, the Church Wardens of every parish . . . provide half a score or twenty quarters of malt . . . which malt being made into very strong ale or beer, it is set to sale, either in the Church or some other place assigned. Then when the Nippitatum, this Huf-Cap (as they call it, and this Nectar of Life) is set abroach . . . he that sitteth the closest to it, and spends the most at it, he is counted the godliest man of all the rest.'

Philip Stubbes *The Anatomy of Abuses* 1583

MAY

Greater Celandine (or Swallow-Wort) flowers, and young swallows hatch.

25

'Celandine is called Chelidonium, from the Greek word Chelidon, which signifies a swallow; because they say that if you put out the eyes of young swallows when they are in the nest, the old ones will recover their eyes again with this herb. This I am confident (because I have tried it) that if we mar the very apple of their eyes with a needle, she will recover them again: but whether with this herb or not, I know not.'

Culpeper *Herbal* 1653

'The juice of this herb is good to sharpen the sight, for it cleanseth and consumeth away slimy things that cleave about the ball of the eye, and hinder the sight.'

Gerard *Herbal* 1633

The orange liquid from the broken stems of Greater Celandine is said to cure warts.

May cheeses now being made.

26

'Cheese that is good ought not to be too hard nor too soft, but betwixt both: it must be of good savour, not full of eyes, nor mites, nor maggots. Yet in High Germany the cheese the which is full of maggots is called there the best cheese, and they will eat the maggots as fast as Englishmen do comfits.'

Andrew Boorde *Dietary of Health* 1547

'If you will have a very dainty Nettle Cheese, which is the finest Summer Cheese which can be eaten . . . as soon as it is drained from the brine, you shall lay it upon fresh Nettles, and cover it all over with the same, and let it ripen therein. Observing to renew your Nettles once in two days, and every time you renew them, to turn the Cheese. Gather your Nettles as much without stalks as may be, and make the bed both under and aloft as smooth as may be: for the fewer wrinkles your Cheese hath, the more dainty is your House-wife accounted.'

Markham *The English Housewife* 1683

27 Tennis now in season.

'The Tennis Court, whereby I would have you to recreate your mind, and exercise your body sometimes: for besides pleasure it preserveth your health, in so far as it moveth every part of the body. Nevertheless I approve not those who are ever in the Tennis Court like Nackets, and heat themselves so much that they rather breed than expel sickness: nor yet commend I those, who rail at the Tennis-keeper's score, and that have banded away the greater part of their wealth in playing great and many sets. It is both a hurt and a shame for a nobleman to be so eager in that play.'
James Cleland *The Institution of a Young Noble Man* 1607

'The Earl of Leicester, being very hot and sweating, took the Queen's napkin out of her hand and wiped his face: which the Duke of Norfolk seeing said that he was too saucy, and swore that he would lay his racket about his face. Here upon rose a great trouble, and the Queen offended sore with the Duke.'
Report of a tennis match before Queen Elizabeth, 1565

28 Make Whitsun cheese-cakes.

'To make Cheese-cakes. Take twelve pints of Milk warm from the Cow and turn it with a good spoonfull of Rennet. Break it well, and put it into a large strainer, in which roll it up and down, that all the Whey may run out. Then break the Curds and wring it again, and more Whey will come, and so break and wring till no more will come. Work the Curds exceedingly with your hand in a tray, till they become a short uniform Paste: then put to it the yolks of eight new laid Eggs, two whites, and a pound of butter. Work all this long together, for in the long working consisteth the making them good. Then season them to your taste with Sugar finely beaten, and put in some Cloves and Mace in subtle powder: lay them thick in Coffins of fine Paste, and so bake them.'
The Closet of Sir Kenelm Digby Opened 1669

Oak Apple Day.

29

This is the anniversary of the Restoration of Charles II, who entered London in triumph on May the twenty-ninth (also his birthday) in 1660. The oak leaves and 'oak apples' traditionally worn today commemorate Charles's 'miraculous' escape after his defeat at Worcester in 1651, when he hid from parliamentarian troops by hiding in an oak tree.

Long before 1660, Charles had been crowned King of Scots: and on hearing of his Restoration in England, Margaret Dixon of Newcastle remarked: 'What, can they find no other man to bring in than a Scotsman? What, is there not some Englishman more fit to make a King than a Scot? There is none that loves him but drunk whores and whoremongers. I hope to see his bones hanged at a horse's tail, and the dogs run through his puddings.'

York Castle Trial Records, 1660

30

Beware of shrews: cure bed-wetting, possibly caused by picking Dandelions, alias Piss-a-Beds.

'The Shrew Mouse, which is a mouse with short uneven legs and a long head like a swine's, is venomous, and if it bite a beast the sore will swell and rankle, and put the beast in danger. If it only run over a beast, it feebleth his hinder parts and maketh him unable to go. When a beast be shrew-run, you shall beat him with a bramble which groweth at both ends into the ground.'

Markham *Cheap and Good Husbandry* 1607

'When a young body doth piss in his bed either oft or seldom: if ye will help him take the bladder of a goat, and dry it to powder, and give it him to drink with wine. Or else take the beans (or hinder fallings) of a goat, and give him of the powder in his meat morning and evening, a quarter ounce at every time.'

John Hollybush *The Homish Apothecary* 1561

31

Elderflowers now in bloom for remedies and wines: but avoid using elderwood for any purpose whatever.

'Water of elder flowers for a pure complexion, and against insect biting. Take the flowers off the stalks and pack them down hard in your pan, and then pour on enough boiling water to cover them: cover your pan with a cloth and so let it stand a day and a night, and then strain it.'

Mrs Harrington's Book, 18th century

Elderwood, however, is a useless and dangerous timber: for Judas hanged himself on an elder, and some say that Christ's cross was made from elder – or 'bourtree' in Scots – since which time the tree has been cursed with a foul smell and bent, fragile branches. Elderwood cradles cause children to sicken or die: and if even the smallest quantity of elder is burned in the fire, the Devil will come and sit on the chimney.

JUNE
THE MIDSUMMER MONTH

Named after Juno, the great Roman goddess of the moon, of
women, and of childbirth.

In Welsh: *Mehefin* – Midsummer.

In Gaelic: *An t'Og mhios* – the young month.

In Anglo-Saxon: *Litha* – the month of the Midsummer moon.

1

A hot month is to be expected, and a wet one is good for crops.

A dry May and a rainy June
Puts the farmer's pipe in tune.

June damp and warm
Doth the farmer no harm.

'A Spinnach Sallet boiled. Parboil spinnach, and chop it fine with the back of two chopping knives: then set it on a chafing dish of coals with Butter and Vinegar. Season it with Cinnamon, Ginger, Sugar and a few parboiled Currants. Cut hard eggs into quarters to garnish it withal, and serve it upon sippets of toast.'
The Newe Book of Cookerie 1615

2

St Elmo's Day: seek cures for internal ailments.

According to legend, St Elmo or Erasmus was a Syrian bishop, martyred by having his intestines drawn from his body with a windlass or capstan. He is therefore invoked against all stomach and bowel troubles, while his capstan makes him a patron of sailors: 'St Elmo's Fire', the electrical discharges which flicker round ships during storms, is said to be a sign of his protective presence.

'For the Belly Griped. Take a little quantity of the earth that worms cast up out of the ground (which most commonly you shall find in some soft pathway) and mingle therewith a little quantity of Honey. Give the patient half a spoonful in the morning and cause him to fast two hours after: four mornings eating thereof will certainly help.'
Lady Rachel Fane's Book, *c.* 1630

'I do remember that in the great and boisterous Storm, in the Night there came upon the top of our Main Yard and Main Mast a certain little light, much unto the light of a little Candle, which the Spaniards call Corpo Santo and others St Telmes Fire. This light continued about three hours, flying from Mast to Mast and Top to Top; and sometimes it would be in two or three places at once.'
Hakluyt *Voyages* 1598

JUNE

Learning to swim now seasonable: but keep knowledge of your skill from non-swimmers in case of shipwreck.

'In the place of swimming is two things especially to be respected: first, that the banks be not overgrown with rank thick grass, where oft-time do lie and lurk many stinging Serpents and poisoned Toads. . . . Next that the water it self be clear, not troubled with any kind of slimy filth, which is very infectious to the skin; that the breadth depth and length thereof be sufficiently known, and that it be not muddy at the bottom. . . . Then let him associate himself with someone that is taller and stronger than himself, which may both comfort him and help to sustain him: for that at the first entrance the chillness of the water will greatly discomfort him. For the manner of his going into the river, it must not be sweating (a thing whereunto in the heat of the Summer men are greatly subject) for that coming into the cold water it maketh a sudden change in body, which is very dangerous.'

Christopher Middleton *A Short introduction for to learn to Swim* 1595

'I have known many excellent swimmers, whereof some in the sight of the wished Land have perished by the Sea waves, and others have sunk by the weight of their fearful companions knowing their skill.'

Fynes Moryson *Itinerary* 1617

Gather and dry herbs this month.

'Of leaves, choose only such as are green, and full of juice, and cast away such as are any way declining, for they will putrefy the rest. Dry them well in the sun (and not in the shade, as the saying of physicians is): for if the Sun draw away the virtues of the herb, it must needs do the like by hay . . . which the experience of every country farmer will explode for a notable piece of nonsense. Having well dried them, put them up in brown paper, sewing the paper up like a sack, and press them not too hard together, and keep them in a dry place near the fire.'

Culpeper *English Physician* 1653

JUNE

5

Wash sheep and then shear them: but carefully, lest you damage their skin or infect it.

Wash sheep (for the better) where water doth run
And let him go cleanly and dry in the sun
Then shear him and spare not, at two days an end
The sooner, the better his corps will amend.

Reward not thy sheep (when ye take off his coat)
With twitches and patches as broad as a groat
Let not such ungentleness happen to thine
Lest fly with her gentles do make it to pine.

Tusser *Five Hundred Points of Good Husbandry* 1573

'Keep your washed sheep as much from Paths and frequented Roads as possible: for altho' some pretend that the Sand makes the Wool weigh more, it is a cheat, and makes it shear the worse, and what is got that way, may soon be lost in the Life of the Sheep – for the Workman finding double the Trouble, will soon grow careless of their Hides.'

Hillman *Tusser Redivivus* 1710

6

The beautiful and all-curing rose now beginning to bloom.

'The Rose doth deserve the chief and prime place among all flowers whatsoever: being not only esteemed for his beauty, virtues and his fragrant and odoriferous smell; but also because it is the honour and ornament of our English Sceptre, as by the conjunction appearing, in the uniting of those two most Royal Houses of Lancaster and York.'

Gerard *Herbal* 1633

'The juice ought to be pressed out of tender roses, after that which is named the nail be cut away: for that part it is which is white in the leaf. The rest should be pressed and bruised in a mortar in the shadow until it be growen together, and so should it be laid up for eye medicines. . . . It is good for the headache, the ache of the eyes, of the ears, of the gums, of the fundament, of the right gut, and of the mother.'

William Turner *Herbal* 1568

JUNE

Whitsun falls in early June when Easter is late: lamb now in high season.

7

'Whatsoever a man doth ask of God upon Whitsunday morning, at the instant when the Sun arise and play, that will God grant.'

'A Carbonado of Mutton or Lamb. Take Mutton or Lamb that hath either been roasted or but parboiled, and with your knife scotch it many ways: then lay it in a deep dish, and put to it a pint of white wine, and a little whole Mace, a little sliced Nutmeg and some Sugar, with a lump of sweet butter, and so stew it till it be very tender. Then take it forth, and brown it on the Grid iron; and then laying sippets of toast in the broth, serve it up.'

Markham The English Housewife 1683

'Do not venture to eat Meat so hot, that the tears stand in your eyes, for that thereby you betray your intolerable greediness: neither fill your mouth so full, that your cheeks shall swell like a pair of Scotch bagpipes. Gnaw no bones with your teeth, nor suck them to come at the marrow.'
Hannah Woolley *The Gentlewoman's Companion* 1675

Observe the Moon and the weather.

8

> If on the eighth of June it rain
> That fortells a wet harvest, men sayen.

'If when you see the new Moon appear, you perceive that some part of her horns are obscured, or if she be black or discoloured in her midst. If she hang much to the West; if she be compassed about either with thick or waterish transparent vapours; of if she look more than ordinarily pale, all these are infallible signs of Rain. And if it beginneth to rain small and mist-like on the fourth or fifth day of the Moon's age, the Rain will continue all that quarter of the Moon following.'

Markham The English Husbandman 1635

The laughing call of the Green Woodpecker – alias Yaffle or Rainbird – is a sure sign of a shower.

9

St Columba's Day: the luckiest day of the year in Highland Scotland, especially when it falls on a Thursday.

> Day of Colum Cille the beloved
> Day to put the loom to use
> Day to put sheep to pasture
> Day to put coracle on the sea
> Day to bear, day to die
> Day to make prayer efficacious
> Day of my beloved, the Thursday.
>
> *Carmina Gadelica*

St Columba's herb is the St John's Wort; if found accidentally and kept beneath the armpit (where the saint is said to have worn it) this will ward off all kinds of evil. Say this charm when you pick it:

> Arm-pit package of Columba the kindly
> Unsought by me, unlooked for
> I shall not be carried away in my sleep
> Neither shall I be pierced with iron
> Better the reward of its virtues
> Than a herd of white cattle.

10

To be rid of undergrowth, cut it in June: but be careful how you deal with knives and other sharp tools.

If you give a knife, a pair of scissors, or any sharp-edged instrument as a present, the recipient must 'buy' it from you with a small coin or a pin: otherwise the gift will sever the friendship between giver and receiver.

'It is thought very ill luck of some, that a child or any other living creature should pass between two friends as they walk together; for they say it portendeth a division of friendship.'

Reginald Scot *Discovery of Witchcraft* 1584

A knife dropped on the floor foreshows a male visitor, a dropped fork a female. But it is unlucky to pick up a knife you have dropped yourself: someone else must do it for you.

Never cross two knives, or lay a knife and fork crosswise: lest 'crosses' (or troubles) follow.

St Barnabas's Day: make Barnaby garlands.

11

> Barnaby bright, Barnaby bright
> Light all day and light all night.

St Barnabas is invoked as a peacemaker and for the amicable settling of disputes. In the pre-1752 'Old Style' calendar his feast fell eleven days 'later' and thus coincided with the Summer Solstice, hence the rhyme.

On this day it was customary to deck churches and houses with Barnaby garlands of Roses and Sweet Woodruff.

'The flowers of woodruff are of a white colour and a very sweet smell: as is the rest of the herb, which being made up into garlands or bundles, and hanged up in houses in the heat of Summer, doth very well attemper the air, cool and make fresh the place, to the delight and comfort of such as are therein.'

Gerard *Herbal* 1633

> When Barnabas smiles both night and day
> Poor Ragged Robin blooms in the hay.

The pink Ragged Robin, alias 'Wild Williams', was also used in Barnaby garlands.

The greatest of summer horse fairs, at Appleby-in-Westmorland, is held during this week.

12

> O there's a horse I bought and sold
> A stallion, colt or brood mare
> I bought her in the winter time
> And sold her at the horse fair.
>
> At Barnet and at Appleby
> They know me well in season
> You'll always find me at Brough Hill
> Likewise at Kirby Stephen.

'To know whether a Horse be sound inwardly, or not. Take his water into a Basin, and behold the colour of it. If it be pale-coloured, whitish or yellow, that is a good sign . . . but if it be either very . . . clear, or of some strong colour like March beer, he is troubled with some disease.'

Crowshey *The Good Husband's Jewell* 1651

> One white leg, buy a horse
> Two white legs, try a horse
> Three white legs, shy a horse
> Four white legs, shoot a horse.

JUNE

13

St Antony of Padua, whose feast day this is, is invoked for the finding of lost property: try divination by the sieve and shears, or by the bible and key.

'The Magic of the Sieve and Shears. The Shears are stuck in the wood of the Sieve, and two maidens hold up the sieve with the top of their fingers by the handle of the shears. Then say, "By St. Peter and St. Paul, such a one hath stolen such a thing": and others say, "By St. Peter and St. Paul, he hath not stolen it." After many such adjurations, the Sieve will turn at the name of the Thief.'

John Aubrey *Remains of Gentilism* 1688

To find out a thief by the key and bible. Fasten a key into a bible, or book of Psalms, at the words 'If thou sawest a thief, thou didst consent to him' in the fiftieth Psalm. Then write out the names of persons suspect on several pieces of paper, and put these in order into the hollow pipe of the key. When the thief's name is put in 'the Book will wag, and fall out of the Fingers of them that hold it'.

14

Anniversary of the Parliamentarian victory at Naseby, 1645: young squirrels taken now make good pets.

'One that I knew, that was at the Battle of Dunbar, told me that Oliver was carried on with a Divine Impulse: he did Laugh so excessively as if he had been drunk, his Eyes sparkled with Spirits. He obtained a great Victory; but the Action was said to be contrary to human Prudence. The same fit of Laughter seized Oliver Cromwell, just before the Battle of Naseby.'

John Aubrey *Miscellanies* 1695

'Squirrels grow exceedingly tame and familiar to men, if they be accustomed and taken when they are young: for they run up on men's shoulders and will oftentimes sit on their heads, creep into their pockets for nuts, go out of doors and return again home. They are very harmful, and will eat all manner of woolen garments: yet if it were not for this discommodity, they were sweet-sportful beasts and very pleasant playfellows in a house. Their flesh is sweet, but not very wholesome.'

Edward Topsell *History of Four-footed Beasts* 1607

JUNE

St Vitus's Day: seek cures for epilepsy and St Vitus's Dance.

15

The obscure St Vitus was apparently a fourth-century martyr from southern Italy. Because angels danced for him while he was in prison, he is the patron of dancers, actors, and mummers: and via more convoluted reasoning is invoked against epilepsy, chorea (or 'St Vitus's Dance') and other fit-producing diseases. He is also the helper of those who find difficulty in rising early.

'There were from far countries certain men brought into our parts of the world, who when they saw men dance, ran away marvellously afraid: crying out and thinking them to have been mad. And no marvel, for who seeing them leap, skip and trip like Goats and Hinds (if he never saw them before) would not think them either mad, or possessed with some Fury?'

Philip Stubbes *The Anatomy of Abuses* 1583

The red-stalked Herb Robert now blooms around houses: but beware how you treat it, for it is Robin Goodfellow's flower.

16

To wantonly destroy Herb Robert – alias Adder's Tongue and Death-Come-Quickly – is to court snakebite or even worse disasters. Also called Poor Robert, Robin Hood or Robin-in-the-Hedge, it is under the protection of the household goblin Robin Goodfellow or Puck: and like him, it will help you – especially by staunching wounds – if it is well treated.

'Your grandam's maids were wont to set a bowl of milk before him . . . for grinding of malt or mustard, and sweeping the house at midnight. He would chafe exceedingly, if the maid or the goodwife of the house, having compassion of his nakedness, laid any clothes for him. For in that case he sayeth. "What have we here? Hempen, Hampen, here will I never more tread nor stampen."'

Reginald Scot *Discovery of Witchcraft* 1584

17

Make good use of summer fruit, now beginning to be abundant.

'Suppose your stock of children too large; and that, by your care for their support, you should be abridged of some of your own luxuries and pleasures. To make away with the troublesome and expensive brats, I allow, would be the desirable thing: but the difficulty is, how to effect this without subjecting yourself to that punishment which the law has thought proper. On no account miss that useful season the summer, in which you may give your children as much fruit as they can cram down their throats: then be sure not to contradict the poor little things if they choose to play about and overheat themselves in the middle of the day; and afterwards should choose to cool their limbs, by sprawling about after the dew is fallen. If they should chance, after all this, to outlive the month without the worms, a fever, or a general corruption of the blood, you must wait the event of another summer.'
Jane Collier *The Art of Ingeniously Tormenting* 1753

18

Very hot weather now seasonable: guard against sunburn and sore feet.

'To take away freckles or the Sun burning. Steep a piece of Copper in the Juice of Lemon till it be dissolved, and anoint the place with a feather morning and evening, washing it off with white wine.'
The Compleat Cook 1671

'The decoction of the herb called Lady's Bedstraw, being yet warm, is of admirable use to bathe the feet of Travellers . . . and for Lackeys . . . whose long running causeth not only weariness but stiffness . . . to both of which this herb is so friendly, that it makes them to become so lissom, as if they had never been abroad.'
William Coles *Adam in Eden* 1657

'If your face be troubled with heat, take Elder-flowers, Plantain, white Daisy root and Herb Robert, and put these into running water, and wash your face there-with at night and in the morning.'
Hannah Woolley *The Gentlewoman's Companion* 1675

19

Both the native wild strawberry and the larger garden variety – descended from imported New World strains – now fruiting.

'The water of these strawberries distilled is a sovereign remedy and cordial in the palpitations of the heart, that is the panting and beating thereof.'
William Coles *Adam in Eden* 1657

'A tart of Strawberries. Pick and wash your Strawberries clean, and put them in the pastry one by another, as thick as you can. Then take Sugar, Cinnamon and a little Ginger finely beaten, and well mingled together, and cast them on the Strawberries. Cover them with the lid finely cut into Lozenges, and so let them bake a quarter of an hour.'
Thomas Jenner *A Book of Fruits and Flowers* 1653

'Raw cream, eaten with strawberries, is a rural man's banquet: yet I have known such banquets hath put men in jeopardy of their lives, by the excess thereof.'
Andrew Boorde *Dietary of Health* 1547

20

With Midsummer Eve so close, be sure to keep your house clean.

'They were wont to please the Fairies (that they might do them no shrewd turns) by sweeping clean the Hearth, and setting by it a dish whereon was set a mess of milk sopped with white bread: and did set their Shoes by the fire, and many times on the morrow they should find a threepence in one of them. But if they did speak of it they never had any again.'
John Aubrey *Remains of Gentilism* 1688

Farewell, Rewards and Fairies
Good Housewives now may say
For now foul Sluts in Dairies
Do fare as well as they
And though they sweep their Hearths no less
Than Maids were wont to do
Yet who of late for Cleanliness
Finds six-pence in her Shoe?
Richard Corbet *The Faeryes Farewell* c. 1625

21

The Summer Solstice, and the longest day of the year: seek out St John's Wort against Midsummer Eve.

'The virtue of St John's Wort is thus. If it be put in a man's house, there shall come no wicked sprite therein.'

Banckes *Herbal* 1525

'A House (or Chamber) somewhere in London was Haunted; the Curtains would be rashed at Night, and awake the Gentleman that lay there. Henry Lawes to be satisfied did lie with him, and the Curtains were rashed so then: and the Gentleman grew lean and pale with the Frights. One Doctor cured the House of this disturbance . . . the principal Ingredient was Hypericon or John's Wort put under his Pillow.'

John Aubrey *Miscellanies* 1695

If the cuckoo is heard on June the twenty-first, it will be a wet summer.

22

The Sun enters the House of Cancer.

'The man born under Cancer shall be avaricious. He shall love women, be merry, humble, good, wise and well-renowned: but he shall have damage by envy, and strife and discord among his neighbours. He shall have often great fear on the water: he shall find hidden money, and labour sore for his wife. At thirty-three years he shall pass the sea: and shall live seventy years after nature.

'The woman shall be furious, incontinent, soon angry and soon pleased. She shall be nimble, serviceable, wise, joyous, but shall suffer many perils by water: if any person do her a service, she shall recompense them well. She shall be labouring until thirty years, and then have rest. She ought to be married at fourteen years, and shall have many sons. She shall live seventy years.

'As well the man as the woman shall have good fortune, and victory over their enemies.'

Kalendar of Shepheardes 1604

JUNE

Midsummer Eve or Johnsmas Eve, whose night is one of the most uncanny and dangerous of the year.

23

To protect your house, byres and beasts against fairies and evil spirits on Midsummer Eve, gather 'the herbs of St John' before dawn on June the twenty-third, while the dew is still on them. These herbs are St John's Wort, Mugwort, Plantain, Corn Marigold, Dwarf Elder, Yarrow, Ivy, Vervain and Orpins: they should either be made into garlands and hung on the door, or burnt on the Midsummer Fire to drive off the spirits of the air.

'Midsummer Eve is counted or called the Witches' Night: and still in many places on St John's Night they make Fires on the Hills: but the Civil Wars coming on have put all these Rites and Customs quite out of Fashion. Wars not only extinguish Religion and Laws, but also Superstition: and no suffumen is a greater fugator of Phantoms than Gunpowder.'
        John Aubrey *Remains of Gentilism* 1688
Johnsmas Eve Fires should be lit at the moment the sun sets.

At Midnight on Midsummer Eve, walk seven times round a church, clockwise, sowing hempseed and saying:

> Hempseed I sow
> Hempseed I mow
> Let him that is my true love
> Come after me and mow.

Then look over your left shoulder, and you will see the form of your destined lover following you.

Midsummer Day: the Feast of the Nativity of St John the Baptist.

24

St John the Baptist, the herald and precursor of Christ, was born six months before Him (*Luke* I.36), and his nativity is therefore celebrated today, six months before Christmas Eve. Since Christ himself called John 'a burning and a shining light' (*John* V.35) it is also appropriate that he should be commemorated at this Midsummer season; and fortunate for mortals that such a powerful saint watches over this dangerously pagan festival. Because St John's emblem is a lamb, he is a patron of shepherds: and because he lived on 'locusts and wild honey', he protects beekeepers.

25

Make prognostications from the breast and stomach, which are governed by Cancer: and seek cures for them.

'The Breast without hair, signifies a man to be unshamefaced and fearful; the Breast very fleshy, to be inept to learn; hairy on the Breast, to be bold but unconstant. The Belly small, signifieth to be of good capacity; much Hairy from the Navel downwards, to be full of Words; the Belly bearing out big, to be a great feeder.'

The Shepherd's Prognostication 1729

'To help a woman's sore breasts, when they are swelled or else inflamed, take Violet leaves and cut them small, and seeth them in milk or running water with wheat bran or wheat bread crumbs, then lay it to the sore, as hot as the party can endure it.'

Markham *The English Housewife* 1683

26

Soft fruit now plentiful: make the Queen's Sweetmeat with it.

'Marmulate of Cherries with juice of Raspberries and Currants. Mingle juice of Rasps and red Currants with the stoned Cherries, and boil this mixture into Marmulate, with a quarter or at most a third part of Sugar. . . . Madam Plancy (who maketh this sweetmeat for the Queen) useth this proportion. Take three pounds of Cherries stoned: half a pound of clear juice of Raspes, and one pound of the juice of red Currants, with one pound of fine Sugar. Put them all together in the preserving pan; boil them with a quick fire, especially at the first, skimming them all the while as any scum riseth. When you find them of a fit consistence, with a fine clear jelly mingled with the Cherries, take the preserving pan from the fire and bruise the Cherries with the back of your preserving spoon: put them up when they are of a fit temper of coolness. Peradventure, to keep all the year, there may be requisite a little more Sugar.'

The Closet of Sir Kenelm Digby Opened 1669

JUNE

Fairies being particularly active in the period between Midsummer and St Peter's Day, now is a good time to bind them to your service: but if you do see the fairies, be sure you never tell.

27

'An excellent way to get a Fairy. First get a broad square crystal in length and breadth three inches, and lay it in the blood of a white hen three Wednesdays or three Fridays. Then take it out and wash it with Holy Water and fumigate it. Then take three hazel rods of a year's growth, peel them fair and white, and write the fairy's name (which you call three times) on every stick being made flat one side: then bury them under some hill whereas you suppose fairies haunt, the Wednesday before you call her, and the Friday following call her three times at eight or three or ten of the clock. But when you call, be in Clean Life and turn thy face towards the East, and when you have her, bind her in that crystal.'

Elias Ashmole's Manuscripts, late 17th century

Sea travel to foreign parts reckoned to be safe after Midsummer: guard against sea–sickness and outlandish foods.

28

'He that would not vomit at all, let him some days before he take ship, and after at Sea, diminish his accustomed meat, and especially his drink. . . . But I think they do ill, who altogether restrain vomiting, for no doubt that working of the Sea is very healthful. Therefore I advise him to use his accustomed diet till he have sailed a day or two into the Main, and after eating, let him seal his stomach with Marmalade. . . . To restrain the extremity of vomiting, till he be somewhat used to the Sea, let him forbear to look upon the Waves, or much to lift up his head.'

Fynes Moryson *Itinerary* 1617

'Concerning the diet of the French, it is nothing so good or plentiful as ours, they contenting themselves many times with mean Viands. As for the poor peasant, he is fain oftentimes to make up his meal with a Mushroom, or his *Grenoilles* (in English, mere Frogs).'

Henry Peacham *The Compleat Gentleman* 1634

29

St Peter's Day: rushbearings now in full swing.

Good Day to you, you merry men all
Come listen to our rhyme
For we would have you not forget
This is Midsummer time
So bring your rushes, bring your garlands
Roses, John's Wort, Vervain too
Now is the time for our rejoicing
Come along Christians, come along do.

Bishop's Castle Rushbearing Song, Shropshire

Midsummer and St Petertide are the favourite seasons for 'rushbearings', when rushes – or, in the eastern English counties, new-mown hay – are brought in procession to churches and ceremonially strewn there as a floor-covering. In north-western England, particularly, rushcarts with towering flower-bedecked loads of plaited rushes were the focus of the procession, and 'the rushbearing' was the great day of the year.

30

Prepare to begin hay-making: Sir Everard Digby, Gunpowder Plotter, was executed on this day in 1606.

'I would have every good husbandman, about a week after Midsummer, to view his Meadows well. And if he see them turn brown, if the cock heads of the grass turn downwards and stand not upright; if the bells and other vessels of seed stand open and shed their seeds; if your honeysuckles have lost their flowers, and the pennygrass be hard, dry and withered; then shall you well and truly understand that your meadow is ripe and ready to be mown.'

Markham *The English Husbandman* 1635

'Sir Everard Digby was a most gallant Gentleman, and one of the handsomest men of his time. 'Twas his ill fate to suffer in the Powder-plot. When his heart was plucked out by the Executioner (who, after the form, cried "Here is the heart of a Traitor") it is credibly reported he replied, "Thou liest!".'

John Aubrey *Brief Lives* late 17th century

JULY

THE MONTH OF HAYMAKING

Named in honour of Julius Caesar.
In Welsh: *Gorfennaf* – the month of completion.
In Gaelic: *Am Mios buidhe* – the yellow month.
In Anglo-Saxon: *Litha* – the month of the midsummer moon.

1

**If the first of July it be rainy weather
'Twill rain, more or less, for four weeks
together.**

Spells of continuous fair weather now needed to dry out hay and mature growing corn. Yet beware also the ill effects of heat, and the diseases proceeding therefrom.

'In this month use cold herbs and cold meats, abstain from physic, and let the Sun be up ere you walk abroad. In any time of plague or pestilence keep your chamber window shut, opening it when the sun hath force of shining: and be sure to perfume your chambers every evening with tar put on a chafing-dish of coals.'

Neve's *Almanack* 1633

'In this month of July, eschew all wanton bed-sports, and of all things forbear Lettuce.'

Markham *The English Husbandman* 1635

2

Hay making should now be well in hand.

> Let hay still abide
> Till well it be dried
> Then go, Sirs, away
> To ted and make hay
> If storms draweth nigh
> Then 'cock apace' cry.

Tusser *Five Hundred Points of Good Husbandry* 1573

Employ Marsh or Husbandman's Woundwort against wounds sustained in haymaking.

'It chanced that a poor man in mowing . . . did cut his leg with a scythe, wherein he made a wound to the bone, and withal very large and wide, and also with great effusion of blood. The poor man crept unto this herb, which he bruised with his hands, and tied a great quantity of it unto the wound with a piece of his shirt: which presently staunched the bleeding and ceased the pain, insomuch that the poor man presently went to his work again.'

Gerard *Herbal* 1633

JULY

The hot and unhealthy 'Dog Days', when Sirius the Dog Star is in the ascendant, begin today and continue until about August the eleventh.

3

'In these Dog Days it is forbidden by Astronomy to all Manner of People to be let Blood or take Physic. Yea, it is good to abstain all this time from Women. For why, all that time reigneth a Star that is called Canicula Canis, a Hound in English, and the kind of the Star is broiling and burning as Fire. All this time the Heat of the Sun is so fervent and violent that Men's bodies at Midnight sweat as at Midday: and if they be hurt, they be more sick than at any other time, yea very near Dead. In these days all venomous serpents creep, fly and gender, so that many are annoyed thereby; in these times a Fire is good night and day, and wholesome, seeth well your meals and take heed of feeding violently.'

The Husbandman's Practice 1729

Midsummer Eve, Old Style: and thus a good time for making prognostications.

4

'The maids (especially the Cook-maids and Dairy-maids) would stick up in some chinks of the joists Midsummer-men, which are slips of Orpins. They placed them by pairs, one for such a man, the other for such a maid his sweetheart: and accordingly as the Orpin did incline to, or recline from the other, there would be Love or aversion. If either did wither, death.'

John Aubrey *Remains of Gentilism* 1688

Orpine, alias Livelong, will survive for months after picking, because of its fleshy leaves.

'On Midsummer Eve three or four of you must dip your shifts in fair water, then turn them wrong side outwards, and hang them on chairs before the fire, and lay some salt on another chair, and speak not a word. In a short time the likeness of him you are to marry will come and turn your smocks, and drink to you.'

Mother Bunch's Closet c. 1710

5 Old Midsummer Day: beware of being misled by Robin Goodfellow.

> When'er such wanderers I meet
> As from their night-sports they trudge home
> With counterfeiting voice I greet
> And call on them, with me to roam
> Or else, unseen, with them I go
> And frolic it, with Ho! Ho! Ho!
>
> *The Ballad of Robin Goodfellow c.* 1600

'Ho, ho, ho, of Robin Goodfellow. Mr Lancelot Morehouse did aver to me . . . that he did once hear such a Loud Laugh on the other side of a hedge, and was sure that no Human Voice could afford such Laugh.'

John Aubrey *Remains of Gentilism* 1688

To break the fairy spell, turn your coat or cloak inside out.

> Whilst in this mill we labour and turn round
> As in a conjuror's circle, William found
> A means for our deliverance; 'Turn your cloaks'
> Quoth he, for Puck is busy in these oaks.
>
> Corbet *Iter Borealis* 1648

6 Hay-making still in progress in most areas: many rabbits killed by mowers.

A rabbit dish for hay-makers. 'Fit your rabbit for boiling, and seeth it with a little Mutton broth or stock, white wine and a piece of whole Mace: then take Lettuce, Spynach, Parsley, Winter Savory and Sweet Marjoram; all these being picked out and washed clean, bruise them with the back of your ladle (for the bruising of the herbs will make the broth look very pleasantly green). When all is well boiled together, thicken it with a crust of bread, being steeped in some of the broth, and a little sweet butter therein. Season it with verjuice and pepper, and serve it to the table upon Sippets or toasts.'

The Newe Book of Cookerie 1615

Herb Bennet (or Wood Avens) now beginning to seed: use it to combat summer spots.

7

'The stalk of Herb Bennet is round, all hairy and rough, the flower is in some form like a little eye: when the flower is gone there riseth up a great knop all full of little round things like berries of a purple colour. The common property or use of this root is such that if men put it into wine, it maketh it pleasant both in smelling and taste. Many new writers hold the wine wherein this herb is steeped refresheth the heart and maketh it merry. The same wine scoureth out foul spots if the face be bewashed daily therewith.'

William Turner *Herbal* 1568

'It is a most certain truth, that if the second toe, near the great toe, be as long as the great toe, the person will be very rich and happy.'

The New Prognosticater 1690

Frogs now in demand for making love-potions and cures.

8

'The toys which are said to procure love are these. The hair growing in the nethermost part of the wolf's tail, a wolf's yard, the brain of a cat, newt, or lizard. The bone of a green frog, the flesh thereof being consumed by ants, the left bone whereof engendreth love, the bone on the right side, hate. Also it is said of a frog's bones that some will swim and some sink: those that sink being hanged up in a white linen cloth, engender love: but if a man be touched therewith, hate.'

Reginald Scot *The Discovery of Witchcraft* 1584

'To cure the Thrush: Take a living Frog, and hold it in a Cloth, that it does not go down into the Child's mouth: and then put the Head into the Child's mouth till it is dead, and then take another Frog and do the same.'

John Aubrey *Miscellanies* 1695

9

In this season of bathing, note the position of moles on the body.

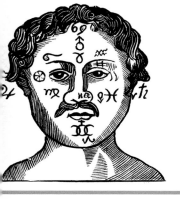

'A mole on the right shoulder, denotes happiness to man or woman; on the left shoulder, a man to be quarrelsome, but a woman to have many husbands; on the left cheek, fruitfullness in man or woman; on the left ribs, a man to be very cruel, a woman vain and proud; on the right breast, denotes a man to be a slave to love, and shows that a woman will be beloved of great Men; under the right loin, signifies an industrious man, and good to a woman; on the buttock, denotes honour to a man, and riches to a woman; on the right side of the belly, denotes a man to flow in riches, and a woman to be happy in marriage; one near the navel signifies many Children.'

The Old Egyptian Fortune-Teller c. 1710

10

Village feasts, fairs and revels now frequent.

'This is to give notice that Yattendon Revel will be kept on the 10th of July, and for the encouragement of gentleman gamesters and others, there will be given an exceedingly good Gold-laced Hat of 27s. value, to be played for at Cudgels, the man that breaks most heads to have the prize. Two shillings will be given to each man that positively breaks a head, for the first ten heads that are broke; the blood to run an inch, or to be deemed No Head.'

Advertisement in the *Reading Mercury* 1782

'To remedy baldness of the head. Take a quantity of Southernwood, and put it on kindled coal to burn: and being made into powder, mix it with the oil of radishes and anoint the bald place, and you shall see great experiences.'

Edward Potter's Phisicke Book, 1610

In Scotland, if it rains today, no less than seven weeks of bad weather are to be expected hereafter.

Both Wild and Sweet Marjoram now in flower.

11

Pleasant-smelling Wild Marjoram, also called Organy and Joy of the Mountain, is a herbal cure-all: made into a tea or infusion, 'It strengthens the stomach and head much, there being scarce a better remedy growing for such as are troubled with a sour humour in the stomach, it restores the appetite being lost; helps the cough and consumption of the lungs; helps the biting of venomous beasts, and such as have poisoned themselves by eating hemlock, henbane, or opium. It provokes urine and the terms in women, helps the dropsy, the scurvy, scabs, itch and yellow jaundice.'
Culpeper *Herbal* 1653

'A pleasant Mead of Sir William Paston's: To a Gallon of water put a quart of honey, about ten sprigs of Sweet-Marjoram; half so many tops of Bays. Boil these very well together, and when it is cold, bottle it up. It will be ten days before it is ready to drink.'
The Closet of Sir Kenelm Digby Opened 1669

Hay now being carted and stacked: be sure it is well dried before you store it.

12

'Hay, if hous'd unmade, is of all Things the most apt to take Fire: what takes Wet by Rain, is not so apt to fire, but it turns to a filthy stinking Mouldiness, that nothing will touch. Coarse and long shady Hay is more coveted by a Cow or Ox, than the best hard Hay: for they having no upper Teeth, cannot chew it so well. Sheep are for the shortest Hay, and are somewhat more nice than Horses: and Horses love the best.'
Hillman *Tusser Redivivus* 1710

'Anno 1670, not far from Cirencester, was an Apparition: Being demanded, whether a good Spirit, or a bad? returned no answer, but disappeared with a curious Perfume and most melodious Twang. Mr W. Lilly believes, it was a Fairy.'
John Aubrey *Miscellanies* 1695

13

**They that wive
Twixt sickle and scythe
Shall never thrive.**

The busy period between hay-making and corn-harvest is esteemed an inconvenient or even unlucky time for marriages.

'A remarkable Superstition still prevails among the lowest of our Vulgar, that a man may lawfully sell his Wife to another, provided he deliver her over with a Halter about her Neck.'

Brand *Observations of Popular Antiquities* 1813

'They came into the market between ten and eleven o'clock in the morning, the woman being led by a halter which was fastened round her neck and the middle of her body. In a few minutes after their arrival she was sold to a man of the name of Thomas Snape, a nailer of Burntwood. The purchase money was 2s. 6d, and all the parties seemed satisfied with the bargain. The husband was glad to get rid of his frail rib, who, it seems, had been living with Snape three years.'

The Wolverhampton Chronicle 1837

14

Red currants now abundant for summer puddings: or make them into jelly, either to eat at once or to keep as a relish with hare.

'Jelly of Red Currants: Take them clean picked and fresh gathered in the morning, in a basin, set them over the fire, that their juice may sweat out, pressing them all the while with the back of your preserving spoon, to squeeze out all that is good. When you see all is out, strain the Liquor from them, and let it stand to settle four or five hours, that the gross matter may sink to the bottom. Then take the pure clear, and to every pint of it, put three quarters of a pound of Sugar, and boil them up with a quick fire, till they come to a jelly height (which will be done immediately in less than a quarter of an hour), which you may try with a drop upon a plate. Then take it off, and when it is cold enough, put it into glasses.'

The Closet of Sir Kenelm Digby Opened 1669

St Swithin's Day, if thou dost rain
Full forty days it will remain
St Swithin's Day, if thou be fair
For forty days, twill rain no mair.

15

The Feast of St Swithin, the most famous of English weather-saints, a humble and much beloved Saxon Bishop of Winchester. On his death-bed, he ordered his body to be buried among the poor in the common churchyard, 'beneath the feet of passers-by and rain from the eaves'. So many miracles occurred at his graveside, however, that the monks moved his remains to a splendid shrine in Winchester Cathedral: whereupon the saint wept in protest, causing a continuous downpour which lasted forty days.

Rain on St Swithin's Day 'blesses and christens the apples', which should not be picked or eaten before his Feast: all apples growing at this time will ripen and come to maturity.

Observe the appearance of new-born babies: and note the first words they speak.

16

A child born with its hands open will grow up generous and benevolent, but one born with clenched fists will be mean. Babies born with hair on their arms and hands, or with a dimple on the chin, will be prosperous, but 'a dimple on the cheek, leaves a fortune to seek'. Children born with teeth will be 'hard-bitten'; and if their eyebrows meet in the middle, they will grow up wrathful.

'Children that cannot speak unto the time that they come to a certain age, yet doth speak these three words: "Ava" doth signify "father"; "Acca" doth signify joy or mirth: "Agon" signifieth dolour or sorrow. All infants speak these words, if a man do mark them: but what "Wa" doth signify when they cry, I never could read of it; if it do signify anything it is displeasure, or not contented.'

Andrew Boorde *Extravagantes* 1547

17

Be careful with salt cellars and wine glasses.

'The falling of salt is an authentic presagement of ill-luck. . . . For Salt as incorruptible was the Symbol of Friendship, and before other service was offered unto their guests.'

Sir Thomas Browne *Pseudodoxia Epidemica* 1646

Some say that 'to help someone to salt is to help them to sorrow': and hold that for a salt cellar to fall towards you is particularly unlucky. The omen may, of course, be averted by throwing some of the spilt salt over your left shoulder, so as to hit the Devil in the eye.

To spill wine at table is also thought ominous, and 'In the eastern ports of England, they hold that should a wine glass or other vessel accidentally ring against another, and the ringing noise not be at once stilled before it comes to its natural conclusion, then that is some poor sailor's death knell: and thus they carefully avoid the same, for fear of causing (as they believe) their neighbours' drowning.'

John Thompson *Mariner's Almanack c.* 1780

18

Cucumber now abundant.

'To Pickle Cucumbers for the winter-time. Put them in an earthenware vessel: lay first a lay of salt and Dill, then a lay of Cucumbers, and so till they be all laid. Put in some Mace and whole Peppers, and some Fennel-Seed: then fill it up with Malt or Beer-vinegar: and put a clean board and a stone upon it to keep them within the pickle, and so keep them close covered.'

The Compleat Cook 1671

On Sunday July the 18th 1652, Mary Fisher of Selby, spinster 'did openly in the parish church speak unto Richard Calvert, minister there, being in the pulpit and preaching, these words. "Come down, come down, thou Painted Beast, come down. Thou art but an hireling, and deludest the people with thy lyes."'

York Castle Trial Records

**Wormwood and many other herbs now begin-
ning to seed.**

While wormwood hath seed, get a handful or twain
To save against March, to make fleas to refrain
Where chamber is swept, and wormwood is strown
No flea, for his life, dare abide to be known.
  Tusser *Five Hundred Points of Good Husbandry* 1573

'Wormwood cleanses the body of choler. It provokes
urine, helps surfeits or swellings in the belly: it causes
appetite to meat. Mix a little Wormwood, an herb of
Mars, with your ink: neither rats nor mice will touch
the paper written with it. Moths are under the
dominion of Mars: this herb Wormwood being laid
among clothes, will make a moth scorn to meddle with
them.'

Culpeper *Herbal* 1653

**The Feast of St Wilgefortis or Uncumber, the
original bearded lady.**

According to legend, Wilgefortis was a daughter of
the King of Portugal, who made a vow of perpetual
virginity: when her father tried to make her marry, she
prayed for deliverance and at once sprouted a copious
beard. Her suitors then fled in horror, and her outraged
father had her crucified. Known in England as
Uncumber or Liberata, she was invoked by women
who wished to 'uncumber' themselves of troublesome
husbands or importunate suitors.

'To know if your husband or wife be bewitched or
not. Look well in their eyes and if you can discern your
picture in them, they are not bewitched: if you cannot
discern your likeness, some person hath bewitched
them.'

Seventeenth-century spell book

21

Heat now encourages restless nights, and many dreams.

'To dream of Eagles flying over our heads, or of Marriages, dancing and banquetting, foretells some of our Kinsfolks are departed; to dream of Silver, if thou hast it given to thyself, is sorrow; of Gold, good fortune; to lose a tooth or an eye, the death of some friend; of bloody Teeth, the death of the dreamer; to weep in Sleep showeth Joy; to see one's Face in the Water, or to see the dead, Long Life; to handle Lead, or to see a Hare, foretells Death.'

The Country-mans Counsellor 1633

'There be some, so curious in telling their dreams from point to point, using such wonder and admiration withall, that it makes a man's heart ache to hear them. And especially because (for the most part) these be such kind of people, as it is but labour lost to hear even the very best exploits they do, when they be most awake.'
Robert Peterson *Treatise of Manners and Behaviours* 1564

22

The Feast of St Mary Magdalen, usually identified with the 'sinful woman' who washed Christ's feet with her repentant tears and dried them with her hair: she is therefore the patron of penitents and of reformed prostitutes.

'The usual canonical penance for a whore hath been, that she shall stand at the church door some hours bare legged and barefoot, in a white sheet, with a candle in her hand. But this is now left off in many places, for they truly say, it but affordeth naughty women of their bodies occasion to display their wares, and entice men to filthiness.'

The Country Justice 1668

Rain today shows that St Mary Magdalen is washing her handkerchief to go to her cousin St James's Fair, in three days time. But heavy rain now can be disastrous for the harvest, and

> A Magdalen Flood
> Never did good

Cumbrian rhyme

Be careful not to overtire horses during hot weather.

23

'If your horse be tired with journeying, your best help for him is to give him warm urine to drink: and letting him blood in the mouth, suffer him to lick up and swallow the same. Then if you can come where any nettles are, to rub his mouth and sheath well therewith: then gently ride him until you come to your resting place, where set him up very warm, and before you go to bed give him six spoonfuls of aqua vitae to drink and as much provender as he will eat.'

Markham *Cheap and Good Husbandry* 1613

'To hinder the Night-mare, they hang in a string a Flint with a hole in it (naturally) by the manger: but best of all they say, hung about their necks. This is to prevent the Night-mare, that is the Hag, from riding their horses, who otherwise will sweat all night.'

John Aubrey *Miscellanies* 1695

The Sun enters the House of Leo.

24

'The man born under Leo shall be hardy, he shall speak openly, and be merciful: but he shall be arrogant in words. At thirty years he shall be damaged, but shall eschew that peril: he shall have goods by temporal services, and as much as he loseth he shall win. He will go often on pilgrimages, and suffer pain of the sight. He shall fall from on high; at thirty-six years he shall be bitten of a dog, and shall live ninety-four years after nature.

'The woman shall be a great liar, fair, well-spoken, pleasant, merciful, and may not suffer to see men weep. Her first husband shall not live long, but she shall live to get great riches, and shall have children of three men. She shall live seventy-eight years after nature.'

Kalendar of Shepheardes 1604

25

An auspicious day for journeys, since it is the feast of two travellers' saints, St Christopher and St James the Greater.

St Christopher, whose name means 'Christ-bearer', was a legendary giant who carried the infant Christ on his shoulders across a rushing torrent: he is therefore the patron of wayfarers, and it was believed that anyone who looked on his image would be preserved from sudden death throughout that day. St James, one of the Twelve Apostles, had his principal shrine at Santiago de Compostela in Spain, a magnet for pilgrims from all over Europe: he is the special protector of pilgrims, who often wore his badge of a Compostela scallop shell.

'In all Inns, but especially in suspect places, let the traveller bolt or lock the door of his chamber: let him take heed of his chamber fellows, and always have his sword by his side; let him lay his purse under his pillow, but always folded with his garters, or some other thing he first useth in the morning, lest he forget to put it up before he go out of his chamber.'

Fynes Moryson *Itinerary* 1617

26

Today is the Feast of St Anne, mother of the Virgin Mary and patron of housewives: treat them to apricot cream-ice.

'To make cream ice. Peel, stone and scald twelve apricots, beat them fine in a mortar, and put to them six ounces of sugar and a pint of scalding cream. Work it through a fine sieve, put it into a tin that hath a close cover, and set it in a tub of ice broken small and a large quantity of salt put among it. When you see your cream grow thick around the edges, stir it and set it in again until it is all frozen up. Then put on the lid and have ready another tub with ice and salt as before: put your tin in the middle and lay ice over and under it: let it stand four or five hours, and then dip your tin in warm water before you turn it out. You may use any sort of fruit if you have not apricots, only observe to work it fine.'

Elizabeth Raffald *The Experienced English Housekeeper* 1769

Beans now ready for gathering: make portable vinegar.

27

'Beans eaten, are extremely windy meat.'
Culpeper *Herbal* 1653

'The Earl of Oxford, making of his low obeisance to Queen Elizabeth, happened to let a Fart, at which he was so abashed and ashamed that he went to travel, seven years. On his return the Queen welcomed him home and said, "My Lord, I had forgot the Fart." '
John Aubrey *Brief Lives* late 17th century

'To make Vinegar which you may carry in your pocket, you shall take the seed of green corn, and beat it in a Mortar with the strongest vinegar you can get. Then roll it into little Balls, and dry it in the Sun till it be very hard. When you have occasion to use it, dissolve a piece in Wine, and it will make strong Vinegar.'
Markham *The English Housewife* 1683

Beware sunstroke, but shun parasols.

28

'In summer, keep your neck and face from the sun, and use to wear gloves made of goatskins. And beware in standing or lying on the ground in the reflection of the sun, but be always movable. If you shall commune or talk with any man, stand not still in one place, especially if it be on the bare ground, or grass, or stones. Also beware in summer that you do not lie in old chambers that be not occupied, specially such chambers as mice, rats and snails resorteth unto.'
Andrew Boorde *Dietary of Health* 1547

'In hot regions, to avoid the beams of the Sun, in some places (as in Italy) they carry Umbrels, or things like a little Canopy over their heads: but a learned Physician told me, that the use of them was dangerous, because they gather the heat into a pyramidal point, and thence cast it down perpendicularly upon the head.'
Fynes Moryson *Itinerary* 1617

29

Strong-smelling meadowsweet, alias Queen of the Meadow, now flowering everywhere in damp places.

'The leaves and flowers far excell all other strewing herbs, for to deck up houses, to strew in chambers, halls and banquetting houses in the Summer time: for the smell thereof makes the heart merry, delighteth the senses. Neither doth it cause headache, or loathsomeness to meat, as some other sweet smelling herbs do.'

Gerard *Herbal* 1633

'A sure medicine for toothache. Take a garlic head, beat it in a mortar that it wax soft: and look on what side or cheek the toothache is. On that arm bind the garlic upon the wrist. Cover it with a broad walnut shell a whole night, and then it will cast a blister: pierce the same through, or else it will burst by itself. That healeth the tooth.'

John Hollybush *The Homish Apothecary* 1568

30

On this day in 1643 died the Earl of Kingston, who had attempted to stand neutral in the Civil War between King and Parliament.

' "When" said he, "I take up arms with the King against the Parliament, or with the Parliament against the King, let a cannon-bullet divide me between them"; which God was pleased to bring to pass a few months after. For he, going to Gainsborough and there taking up arms for the King, was surprised by my Lord Willoughby, and was put prisoner into a pinnace, and sent down river to Hull; when my Lord Newcastle's army marching along the shore, shot at the pinnace, and being in danger, the Earl of Kingston went up on the deck to show himself and to prevail with them to forbear shooting. But as soon as he appeared, a cannon-bullet flew from the King's army and divided him in the middle: and thus, being then in the Parliament's pinnace, he perished according to his own unhappy imprecation.'

Lucy Hutchinson *Memoirs of Colonel Hutchinson* 1664

JULY

Hay-making now generally over, and corn-harvest beginning: field workers must beware lightning.

31

Here lye two poor Lovers, who had the mishap
Tho' very chaste people, to die of a Clap.

Epitaph at Stanton Harcourt, Oxfordshire, allegedly by Alexander Pope, on 'John Hewett and Margaret Drew, an Industrious young man and Virtuous Maiden of this Parish, Contracted in Marriage: who being at Harvest-Work were in one Instant killed by Lightning, the last day of July, 1718.'

'The general profit of Thunder. The effect of Thunder is profitable to men, both for that the sweet shower doth follow it, and also for that it purgeth and purifieth the Air by the swift movement as also by the sound: which, dividing and piercing the Air, causeth it to be much thinner, and therefore the more purer.'

Lake's *Almanack* 1627

AUGUST

THE MONTH OF HARVEST

Named in honour of the deified Roman Emperor Augustus.

In Welsh: *Awst*

In Gaelic: *An Lugnasda* – the month of the Lammas festival.

In Anglo-Saxon: *Weodmonath* – the month of weeds.

AUGUST

Lammas Day; Lugnasadh.

1

Lammas — 'loaf-mass' — is the festival of harvest's beginning, when the first-cut sheaf of corn, or bread made from it, was blessed and offered in churches. 'Lammas Lands', used for growing early crops or hay, are today thrown open for common grazing until next Spring.

In Highland Scotland, Lammastide was 'Lugnasadh' — the festival of the Celtic god Lugh Lightborn, celebrated with gatherings, sports and great bonfires. Like other 'Quarter Days', it is also a time when spirits walk abroad, and hence a good time to divine the future. To learn the whereabouts of your destined lover's home, take a ladybird and address her thus before releasing her:

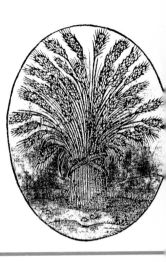

> Lady, Lady Lanners
> Tak your cloak about your heid
> And fly away to Flanders
> Fly ower moor and fly ower mead
> Fly ower living, fly ower dead
> Fly ye east or fly ye west
> Fly to her that loves me best.

Guard your health during sultry August: invaluable feverfew now in flower.

2

Against summer headaches and migraines inhale the crushed leaves of yellow and white feverfew — the 'febrifuge', or fever-chaser. Dried, powdered and taken with honey or sweet wine, 'feverfew purgeth by siege melancholy and phlegm, wherefore it is very good for them that are giddy in the head, or which have the turning called Vertigo, that is a swimming or turning in the head. Also it is good for such as be melancholic, sad, pensive and without speech.'

Gerard *Herbal* 1633

On this day in 1100, King William Rufus was mysteriously slain by an arrow while hunting in the New Forest. Some believe that the notoriously evil-living monarch — who seems to have expected to die on that day — was a Lammas sacrifice to the old gods: but he was more probably killed by order of his brother and successor Henry I.

3

High time to get harvesting under way.

Make sure of thy reapers, get harvest in hand
The corn that is ripe, doth but shed as it stand
Grant harvest lord more, by a penny or two
To call on his fellows the better to do
Give gloves to thy reapers, a largess to cry
And ever to loiterers have a good eye.

Tusser *Five Hundred Points of Good Husbandry* 1573

The harvest lord, or 'King of the Mowers', was the trusted man elected by the harvest-workers to direct operations: the reapers' gloves protected their hands against thistles and 'noisome weeds' among the corn.

On this day in 1719, 'A Woman, who had served the Lady Anne Harvey for about sixteen years in the Quality of a Coachman, and always behaved very well, was brought to bed of a Child, to the Inexpressible Surprize of the Family, who always took her for a Man.'

The Original Weekly Journal 1719

4

'Sunday, being the fourth of August, at a certain town called Bungay, there fell from heaven an exceedingly great and terrible tempest. . . . Immediately hereupon, there appeared in a most horrible similitude and likeness to the congregation, a dog as they might discern it, of a black colour. This black dog, or the Devil in such a likeness, running all along down the body of the church with great swiftness among the people, passed between two persons as they were kneeling upon their knees, wrung the necks of them both at one instant clean backwards, insomuch that they strangely died. The same black dog, passing by another man, gave him such a gripe on the back, that therewithal he was presently drawn together and shrunk up, as it were a piece of leather scorched in a hot fire. . . . Now for the verifying of this report, there are remaining in the stones of the church, and likewise in the church door, the marks as it were of his claws or talons. And besides that all the wires, the wheels and other things belonging to the clock are broken and wrung in pieces.'

A strange and terrible Wunder wrought very late at Bungay
1577

AUGUST

St James's Day, Old Style: traditionally the beginning of the oyster-eating season.

> Greengrocers rise at dawn of sun
> August the fifth – come haste away
> To Billingsgate the thousands run
> Tis Oyster Day! Tis Oyster Day!
> Hone *Every-Day Book* 1829

Londoners believed that whoever ate an oyster today would never want money all the year: but the more usually accepted doctrine is that oysters are only wholesome when there is an 'R' in the month: and thus not until September.

'For deafness. Take a great oyster shell and fill it with fasting spittle, and let it stand two days and nights in a dunghill. Then take it out and put one drop in the ear, and stop it with black wool which is wet likewise with the same.'
Fairfax Household Book, 17th/18th century

Very hot weather now presages a hard winter: Ben Jonson, first Poet Laureate, died on this day in 1637.

'Signs of hot weather. Many bats flying abroad sooner than ordinary. A white mist arising out of moors or waters, either before Sun rising or after Sun setting. Birds flying high in the air. Crows or ravens gaping against the Sun. Store of flies playing in the Sun shining towards night.'
Swallow's *Almanack* 1633

'Ben Johnson, riding through Surrey, found the Women weeping and wailing, lamenting the Death of a Lawyer who lived there. He enquired why so great Grief for the Loss of a Lawyer? O, said they, we have the greatest Loss imaginable; he kept us all in Peace and Quietness, and was a most charitable good Man. Whereupon Ben made this distich:

> God works Wonders now and then
> Behold a Miracle, deny't who can
> Here lies a Lawyer, and an Honest Man.'
John Aubrey *Brief Lives* late 17th century

7 Harvest now well under way, and harvest beer flowing.

'It is a general practise on the first day of Harvest, for the men to leave the field about four o'clock and retire to the alehouse, and have what is here termed a 'whet'; that is a sort of drinking bout to cheer their hearts for labour. They previously solicit any who happen to come within their sight with, "I hope, sir, you will please to bestow a largess upon us?" If the boon is conceded, the giver is asked if he would like to have his largess hallooed; if this is assented to, the men all "holler largess" at the tops of their voices.'

Letter from Norfolk, 1826

'It chanceth sometime to some folk to be drunken and yet do not drink overmuch, and that happeneth two manner of ways. First that they have had so great pain or wept so much that thereby their brains are become feeble: and when they drink the drinking doth so much the sooner strike into their brains. Or else they naturally have a feeble head and brains.'

John Hollybush *The Homish Apothecary* 1561

8 Mustard plants now beginning to seed: cut them down, dry them, and thresh them for seed.

'Mustard is an excellent sauce for such whose blood wants clarifying, and for weak stomachs. The seed taken by itself in an electuary or drink, doth mightily stir up bodily lust, and helps the spleen and pains in the sides, and gnawings in the bowels. Being chewed in the mouth, it oftentimes helps the toothache.'

Gerard *Herbal* 1633

'Mustard is also good to be laid upon the heads of them that have the Drowsy Evil, or forgetful sickness called Lethargies, after that the hair is shaven off.'

William Turner *Herbal* 1568

Observe the Harvest Moon.

9

The Moon doth always piss, when she is pale
When red, she farts: when white, she wipes her tail.

'Countrymen observe as a certain rule, that a dripping
moon (that is, perpendicular) presages wet, especially
the Moon being of a cloudy and blackish colour in a
clear sky; and that the weather will last so a good
while.'

Aubrey Observations c. 1685

'To see the New Moon, for the first time after her
Change, on the right hand or directly before you,
betokens good fortune that month: as to have her on
your left or behind you, so that in turning your head
you happen to see her, foreshows the worst, especially
if you have no money then in your pocket. And to see
the New Moon through glass is exceedingly ill-
omened, though you may somewhat avert bad fortune
by turning over all the money you have.'

Campbell Book of Omens 1730

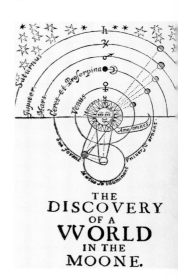

THE
DISCOVERY
OF A
WORLD
IN THE
MOONE.

St Laurence's Day: the cooks' festival

10

St Laurence was a Spanish deacon, supposedly martyred at Rome in 258 by being roasted on a grid-iron.
He is thus the special patron of confectioners, bakers,
and cooks.

'The Cook must be cleanly both in body and
garments. She must have a quick eye, a curious nose, a
perfect taste, and a ready ear; and she must not be
butter-fingered, sweet-toothed, nor faint-hearted. For
the first will let everything fall; the second will
consume what it should increase; and the last will lose
time with too much niceness.'

Markham The English Housewife 1683

On this day in 1787 'Died at Bolton in Lancashire, the
Reverend Richard Godwin of Gateacre. His death is
supposed to have been occasioned by eating too large a
Quantity of Plums the preceding day, after Dinner.'

The Derby Mercury 1787

AUGUST

11

Lammas Eve, Old Style: the last of the hot and unhealthy 'Dog Days', which began on July the third.

Lammas Eve is an uncanny and spirit-haunted time: and in Scotland crosses of rowan wood, sovereign against evil, were fastened above doors and windows this evening, or at latest by noon on Old Lammas Day. This must be done secretly, and the cross-maker must not speak to anyone he meets, or the charm is broken. Cattle may likewise be protected by tying red and blue threads round their tails.

'There is not any creature without reason, more loving to his Master nor more serviceable than is a Dog. In their rage they will set upon all strangers: yet herein appeareth their noble spirit, for if any fall or sit down upon the ground and cast away his weapon, they bite him not. They meet their Master with reverence and joy, crouching or bending a little like shamefast or modest persons: they remember any man which hath given them meat; and when he fawneth on a man he wringeth his skin in the forehead.'
Edward Topsell *History of Four-footed Beasts* 1607

12

Old Lammas Day, the season for trial or 'handfast' marriages in Scotland.

'At the Lammas Fair, it was the custom for unmarried persons of both sexes to choose a companion, according to their liking, with whom they were to live till that time next year. This was called Hand-fasting, or hand-in fist. If they were pleased with each other, then they continued together for life: if not, they separated, and were free to make another choice.'
Old Statistical Account 1794, Parish of Eskdalemuir

'Sir William Roper came one morning, pretty early, to Sir Thomas More, with a proposal to marry one of his daughters . . . who were then both together abed in their father's chamber asleep. He carries Sir William into his chamber and takes the sheet by the corner and suddenly whips it off. They lay on their backs, and their smocks up as high as their armpits. This awakened them, and immediately they turned on their bellies. Quoth Roper, I have seen both sides, and so gave a pat on the buttock he made choice of, saying, Thou art mine. Here was all the trouble of the wooing.'
John Aubrey *Brief Lives* late 17th century

13

The Feast of St Cassian, a severe Christian schoolmaster disliked by his pagan pupils, who stabbed him to death with iron pen-knibs: he is the patron saint of schoolteachers.

Pedantius.

'I had, I remember, myself a Master who by no entreaty would teach any Scholar he had, further than his father had learned before him: as, if the father had only learnt but to read English, the son should go no further. His reason was that they would otherwise prove saucy rogues, and rule their fathers.'

Henry Peacham *The Compleat Gentleman* 1634

'When you are to correct any stubborn or unbroken boy, you must be sure with him to hold him fast. . . . To this end appoint three or four of your scholars, who you know to be honest and strong enough (or more if need be) to lay hands on him together to hold him fast over some form, so that he cannot stir hand or foot; or else if no other remedy will serve, to hold him to some post (which is far the safest and freest from inconvenience).'

John Brinsley *The Grammar Schoole* 1612

14

The flowers of harvest-time – Harvest Bells, Harvest Daisies and Harvest Lilies – all now in bloom.

Harvest Bells are better known as 'Harebells', 'the Bluebells of Scotland'. This flower of the magical hare, also called Fairy Caps and Fairy Ringers, has supernatural protectors, so it is very unlucky to pick it.

More useful, especially for short-breathed or ever-thirsty harvesters, is the Harvest Daisy, alias Dog Daisy.

'The whole Herb, Stalks, Flowers and Leaves, boiled in Posset-drink, is accounted an excellent remedy for an Asthma, Consumption, and Difficulty of Breathing. A Decoction of the Herb cures all Diseases that are occasioned by excessive drinking of cold Beer when the Body is hot.'

John Pechey *The Compleat Herbal of Physical Plants* 1694

Herbalists spoke disparagingly of the Harvest Lily, the common Hedge Bindweed: but harvesters' children amuse themselves by putting its flimsy white bells over their noses, and breathing in to keep them there.

15

The Feast of the Assumption – or death and bodily entrance into Heaven – of the Virgin Mary, called in Scotland 'Great St Mary's Feast in Harvest'.

To make the *Moilean Moire* (Gaelic: 'Mary's Bannock') traditional on this day. Pluck ears of new corn, dry them in the sun, husk them by hand, grind them with stones, knead the flour on a sheepskin, make it into a cake, and toast this by a fire of magical rowan-wood. A piece of the bannock must be eaten by each member of the family in order of age, and all must then walk sunwise round the fire. Finally, gather the embers into a pot, and carry this sunwise round the farm and fields.

> I went sunways round my dwelling
> In the name of Mother Mary
> Who promised to preserve me
> Who did protect me
> Who will preserve me
> In peace, in flocks, in righteousness of heart.
> *Carmina Gadelica*

16

St Roch's Day: take precautions against contagious diseases.

St Roch, a selfless fourteenth-century plague doctor, is invoked against all infectious diseases: his feast day falls at the height of the most dangerous season for epidemics.

'For the Pestilence. Take of Sage, Yarrow, Tansy and Feverfew, of each a handful, and bruise them well together: then let the sick party make water in the herbs, then strain them, and give it to the sick to drink.'
Markham *The English Husbandman* 1635

'It is observed at Plague-times, that the opening of the South-windows brings the sickness; and shutting of the southern windows and opening the northern cures it. Tis said, that drawing in the heat of the fire with one's breath doth much good to him that has the plague.'

John Aubrey *Observations c.* 1685

Time to gather garden seeds: fear rain now to lay unharvested corn.

'Seeds must be gathered in fair weather, at the wane of the Moon, and kept some in Boxes of Wood, some in bags of Leather, and some in Vessels of Earthenware, and well cleansed and dried in shadow. Other some, as Onions and Leeks, must be kept in their husks. It is best to plant in the last quarter of the Moon.'

Markham *The English Housewife* 1683

'Presages of rain: Ducks and Drakes shaking and fluttering their wings when they rise; young Horses rubbing their backs against the ground; Sheep bleating, playing or skipping wantonly; Oxen licking themselves against the hair; the sparkling of a Lamp or Candle; the falling of Soot down a chimney more than ordinary; Frogs croaking; Swallows flying low; the unaccustomed noise of Poultry or cry of Peacocks; Bells heard further than commonly.'

The Husbandman's Practice 1664

St Helena's Day: employ Houseleek against lightning and burns.

St Helena, historically the formidable mother of the Emperor Constantine, is invoked against fire, tempest and lightning.

Also protective against lightning, and useful to cure burns, is the succulent-leaved Houseleek or Sengreen, once carefully cultured on roofs and still found there. 'Old writers do call it Jupiter's Beard, and hold opinion superstitiously that in what house soever it groweth, no Lightning or Tempest can do any harm.'

William Bullein *Book of Simples* 1562

'The leaves of Sengreen by themselves laid to with parched barley meal are good for the burning heat of swelled places called Erisepelata or St Anthony's Fire, against creeping sores, against the inflammation of the eyes, against burnings and hot gouts. Some do use to set it on their roofs.'

William Turner *Herbal* 1568

19

Weigh suspected witches against the Bible: mice now breeding apace.

In August 1759. 'One Susannah Haynokes, an elderly woman of Wingrave near Aylesbury, Bucks, was accused by her neighbour for bewitching her Spinning Wheel, so that she could not make it go round, and offered to make Oath of it before a Magistrate. On which Susannah's husband, in order to justify his wife, insisted on her being tried by the Church Bible, and that the accuser be present. Accordingly she was conducted to the Church, where she was stripped of all her clothes, to her Shift and Under Coat, and weighed against the Bible: when, to the no small mortification of her accuser, she outweighed it, and was honourably acquitted of the Charge.'

The Gentleman's Magazine 1759

'The generation and procreation of Mice is not only by copulation, but also nature worketh wonderfully in engendering them from earth and small showers of rain. . . . A female Mouse having free liberty to litter, within less than half a year she hath brought forth a hundred and twenty young ones.'

Edward Topsell *History of Four-footed Beasts* 1607

20

Revive overworked harvesters: make 'shot' or harvest-drink.

Opera te-
nebrarum.

'For the lethargy, or extreme drowsiness provoked by heat, you shall by all violent means, either by noise or other disturbances, force perforce keep the party from sleeping: and whensoever he calleth for drink, you shall give him White Wine and Hyssop water, of each a little quantity mixed together, and not suffer him to sleep above four hours in four-and-twenty, till he come to his usual wakefulness. Which as soon as he hath received, you shall then forthwith purge his head with the juice of Beets squirted up into his nostrils.'

Markham *The English Housewife* 1683

'To make a harvester's drink called shot. Take a gallon of water, and put a little of it into a pan with half a pound of oatmeal, a pound of sugar, the juice of an orange and a lemon and their rind sliced small. Boil them for ten minutes, then add the rest of the water, take from the fire, and stir well until it is cold.'

Mistress Clark's Book, 18th century

21

In hot weather, use the Silverweed of harvest fields – alias Wild Tansy or Traveller's Ease – against sunburn and sweaty feet.

'The Water of Wild Tansy cleanseth the skin of all discolourings therein, as Sun-burning, as also Pimples, Freckles and the like: but the leaves steeped in white wine or butter-milk is far better; but the best way of all is to steep it in strong white-wine vinegar, the face being often bathed or washed therein.'

William Coles *Adam in Eden* 1657

'It is certain that your carriers wear the leaves of silverweed in their shoes, which keeps them cool and prevents a too immoderate sweating of the Feet, which causes a soreness in them.'

Deering *Catalogus Stirpium* 1738

22

Anniversary of the battle of Bosworth, 1485, when Richard III was defeated and killed by Henry VII.

'In one of the great fields at Warminster in Wiltshire, in the Harvest, at the very time of the Fight at Bosworth Field, there was one of the Parish took two Sheaves, crying "Now for Richard, Now for Henry": at last, lets fall the Sheaf that did represent Richard; and cried "Now for King Henry, Richard is slain". This action did agree with the very Time, Day and Hour. When I was a School-boy, I have heard this confidently delivered, by some Old Men of our Country.'

John Aubrey *Miscellanies* 1695

'Omens from thunder. Sunday's Thunder portends the death of learned men, judges and others; Monday's, the death of Women; Tuesday's, plenty of Grain; Wednesday's, the death of Harlots and other bloodshed; Thursday's, plenty of Sheep and Corn; Friday's, the slaughter of a great Man, and horrible murders; Saturday's, a general pestilent plague and great death.'

Leonard Digges *A Prognostication Everlasting* 1556

23 The Sun enters the House of Virgo.

'The man born under Virgo shall be a good house-holder, ingenious and solicitous to his work, shamefast and of a great courage: but he will soon be angry. Scarcely shall he be a while with his first wife. He shall be in peril by water, he shall have a wound with iron, and shall live seventy years after nature.

'The woman shall be shamefast, ingenious and painstaking. She ought to be wed at twelve years, but she shall not be long with her first husband. Her life shall be sometime in peril: she shall have dolour at ten years, and if she scape shall live seventy years. She shall bring forth virtuous fruit, and everything shall favour her.

'Man and woman both shall suffer many temptations: they shall delight to live in charity, but they shall suffer much, wheresoever it be.'

Kalendar of Shepheardes 1604

24 Bartlemas, the Feast of St Bartholomew the Apostle.

St Bartholomew, according to legend, was martyred by being skinned alive. Hence he is the patron of butchers, skinners, tanners, bookbinders and all leatherworkers.

This day, famous for its fairs – like the great Bartholomew Fair at Smithfield in London – was long known as 'Black Bartholomew', in remembrance of the wholesale massacre of French Protestants in Paris on August the twenty-fourth 1572.

If Bartlemas Day be fine and clear
You may hope for a prosperous Autumn that year.

Some say that St Bartholomew brings in the cooler Autumn weather – 'St Bartholomew, brings the cold dew' – and that his day ends the forty days of rain presaged by a wet St Swithin's.

All the tears St Swithin can cry
St Barthelmy's mantle can wipe dry.

Seek cures for diseases of the womb, thighs and inward parts, which are governed by Virgo.

25

'If a person either man or woman hath a griping in his guts, especially the fretting of the great gut, take a bundle of raw hemp thread and seeth it in water wherein are many ashes, and so lay it warm to the belly. But if ye have no hemp, then do as I did when I was called to a Woman that was at the point of Travailing, and had so great pain in her belly that the Child leapt up and down, so that all they that were about her were struck astonished. I bound both her legs above the knees hard and fast with a band, and so left it an Ave Maria while, and then loosed it and bound it again, until the pain was wholly taken away.'
John Hollybush The Homish Apothecary 1561

'For the Emrods or Piles: Set a chafing-dish of coals under a close-stool chair, and strew Amber beaten in fine powder upon the coals, and sit down over it, that the smoke may ascend up into the place grieved.'
Thomas Jenner A Book of Fruits and Flowers 1653

Harvest by now well advanced: make strengthening pottage for harvest workers.

26

Reap well, scatter not, gather clean that is shorn
Bind fast, shock apace, have an eye to thy corn
Tusser Five Hundred Points of Good Husbandry 1573

'A good Ordinary Pottage. Take the fleshy and sinewy part of a leg of Beef, and scrag ends of necks of Veal and Mutton. Put them in a ten-quart pot, and fill it up with water: begin to boil about six o'clock in the Morning, to have your Pottage ready for Noon. When it is well skimmed, put in two or three large onions in quarters, and half a loaf (in one lump) of light French bread – all of which will be clean dissolved in the broth. Likewise put in store of good herbs, as Borage, Bugloss, Purslain, Sorrel, Endive or what you will, and season with Salt, Pepper and a very few Cloves. Order it so that the broth be very strong and good, to which end you may after four hours boil a Hen or Capon in it.'
The Closet of Sir Kenelm Digby Opened 1669

27

Wild Poppies – also called Cornroses and Har-vesters – growing everywhere among the corn.

Some hold that to stare too long at wild poppies brings blindness (whence they are locally named Blind Eyes or Blindy-buffs) and that to pick them brings storms, hence their aliases of Lightnings and Thundercups. But for all that, they are nothing like so dangerous a plant as the Black (or Opium) Poppy.

'The common nature of all kinds of Poppy is to cool, wherefore if the heads and leaves be boiled in water it will make a man sleep, if his head be bathed therewith. The juice of Black Poppy, called Opium, assuages aches, brings sleep, and helpeth them that have the Flux. But if a man take too much, it taketh a man's memory away and killeth him. He that hath taken Opium hath a great sluggishness, and all the body is cumbered with a great itch. If the patient be too much sleepy, put stinking things into his nose to wake him therewith: and if his itch continue, put him in a warm bath.'

William Turner *Herbal* 1568

28

On this day in 1770, at Cambridge: 'A country lad, about sixteen, for a trifling wager, ate at a public house in this town, a leg of mutton which weighed near eight pounds, besides a large quantity of bread, carrots, etc. The next night, the cormorant devoured a whole cat smothered with onions.'

The Cambridge Chronicle 1770

'The Flesh of Cats can seldom be free of poison, by reason of their daily food, eating Rats, Mice, Wrens and other birds which feed on poison: and above all the brain of a Cat is most venomous, for it being above all measure dry, stoppeth the animal spirits, by reason whereof memory faileth, and the infected person falleth into a Phrensy. In Spain and Gallia Narbonense they eat Cats, but first of all take away their head and tail, and hang the flesh a night or two in the open air to exhale the poison of it, then finding the flesh to be almost as sweet as a coney.'

Edward Topsell *History of Four-footed Beasts* 1607

The Commemoration of the Beheading of St John the Baptist, executed by the tyrant Herod at the instigation of the dancing girl Salome.

29

'All mixed, effeminate, lascivious, amorous dancing is utterly unlawful to Christians, to chaste and sober persons. For if Herod with but seeing Salome dance was so inflamed by her love, that he promised to give her whatsoever she desired . . . what would he have promised, had he danced with her? And I have heard many impudently say, that they have chosen their Wives, and Wives their Husbands, by dancing. Which plainly proveth the Wickedness of it.'

Philip Stubbes *The Anatomy of Abuses* 1573

'We must also beware that we do not sing, and especially alone, if we have an untuneable voice, which is a common fault with most men. And yet, he that is of nature least apt unto it, doth use it most often.'

Robert Peterson *A Treatise of Manners & Behaviours* 1576

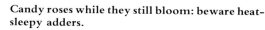
30

Candy roses while they still bloom: beware heat-sleepy adders.

'How to preserve whole Roses or Gilliflowers or Marigolds. You must first pick the seeds out before they do shed. Then dip the flower in Syrup consisting of Sugar Candy boiled, and open the leaves one by one with a smooth bodkin of bone or wood, and as soon as they be dipped lay them in the Sun when it is in the height, or else dry them between two dishes upon papers over a very gentle Fire: and so you may keep them all the year.'

Fairfax Household Book, 17th/18th century

'The greatest injury that adders do us, is in biting Children and Cattle. They affect Milk above anything; and, as old Authors say, abominate the Ash: these then you may use, the one by placing of it hot in any place where they frequent, to attract them where you may destroy them: the other by laying Ashen sticks in the places you would not have them come. But the most proper remedy against these Vermin is to keep Peacocks, which prey on them.'

Worlidge *Systema Agriculturae* 1697

31

With harvest coming to an end, do not hinder gleaners from gathering the corn dropped in the field.

'And when ye reap the harvest of your land, thou shalt not make clean riddance of the corners of thy field when thou reapest, neither shalt thou gather any gleaning of thy harvest: thou shalt leave them unto the poor and the stranger.'

Leviticus XXIII 22

On this day in 1810, 'Eliza Hancock, while gleaning in a field in the parish of Box, near Bath, was accused of stealing wheat from the sheaves, which she denied, and wished she might be struck dead if she had. She was found dead in the field about two hours after.'

The Stamford News 1810

According to tradition, this is the date on which 'The Dove returned to the Ark, with an olive leaf in her mouth'.

SEPTEMBER

HARVEST-HOME, HOPS AND APPLES

The seventh month of the Roman calendar.
In Welsh: *Medi* – the month of reaping.
In Gaelic: *An Sultuine* – the month of plenty.
In Anglo-Saxon: *Halegmonath* – the holy month.

1

Fair weather first day of September, fair for the month.

> This month thou mayest Physick take
> And bleed and bathe for thy health's sake
> Eat figs, and grapes, and spicery
> For to refresh thy members dry.
>
> Neve's *Almanack* 1633

The Feast of St Giles, traditionally a seventh-century hermit of Provence: famous for his pet hind, which he miraculously saved from hunters by causing thick bushes to spring up round them. The special patron of cripples.

Many fairs held on this day, notably St Giles's Fair at Oxford, one of the oldest surviving British fairs: and Eccles Wake in Lancashire, for which the famous Eccles Cakes were originally made.

2

Last corn of harvest now being cut.

In the days of harvesting with hand tools, the 'Last Sheaf' of standing corn was always treated with great reverence, especially in northern and western Britain. There it was known by many honorific titles: the Maiden or the *Cailleach* (old woman) in Scotland; the Neck or Gander's Neck in western England; the Mare in Herefordshire; and the *Caseg Fedi* (harvest mare) or *Gwrach* (hag) in Wales.

The Last Sheaf had to be cut in a particular manner. In Scotland, it was reaped by the youngest maiden or the youngest lad on the farm, and must not touch the ground before being carried home in triumph. But in western England and Wales the standing corn was plaited together, and all the reapers threw their sickles at it until one cut it down, whereupon he cried that he had 'got the Mare' or 'cut the Gander's Neck'.

However it was cut, the Last Sheaf was often dressed in women's clothes, or plaited into a 'Corn Dolly': 'she' then presided over the Harvest Home feast and was carefully kept for luck until the next harvest time.

Reckoned by astrologers to be a day of wonders and marvels, mostly fearful ones.

3

'The Third of September was a remarkable day to the English Attila, Oliver Cromwell. In 1650 he then obtained a memorable Victory over the Scots at Dunbar, and another at Worcester on that day in 1651. And that day he died, 1658.'

John Aubrey *Miscellanies* 1695

Cromwell's death was preceded by the worst storm of the seventeenth century:

> Tossed in a furious hurricane
> Did Oliver give up his reign.

On September the Third 1666, moreover, the Great Fire of London reached its height: and on the same day in 1675 Northampton was 'near burnt down to the ground'.

'Mrs Cromwell's Green Sauce for a Hen or for Bacon: Take a handful of Sorrel, beat it in a mortar with pippin apples pared and quartered, and add thereto a little vinegar and sugar. Otherwise take Sorrel, beat it and stamp it well in a mortar and squeeze out the juice of it: and put thereto a little sugar, vinegar and two hard boiled eggs minced small, a little butter and a grated nutmeg. Set this upon the coals until it is hot, then pour it into the dish upon the roast hen.'

The Court and Kitchen of Elizabeth Cromwell 1664

St Bartholomew's Day, Old Style: harvest-end fairs and wakes now in full swing.

4

Calendar Riot Day. In 1751 Parliament decreed that Britain should change from the 'Old Style' Julian to the 'New Style' (and present) Gregorian Calendar, which was eleven days 'ahead'. To make up the discrepancy, in 1752 September the 2nd was immediately followed by September the 14th: this not unnaturally outraged the London mob, who went on the rampage, demanding 'Give Us Back Our Eleven Days'.

5

'Last Loads' of harvested corn now being brought home in 'Hock Carts', amid much rejoicing.

> The harvest swains and wenches bound
> For joy to see the hock-cart crown'd
> About the cart hear how the rout
> Of rural younglings raise the shout
> Some bless the cart; some kiss the sheaves
> Some prank them up with oaken leaves
> While other rusticks, less attent
> To prayers than to merryment
> Run after with their breeches rent.
>
> Herrick *The Hock Cart* 1648

In the Scottish Highlands, young girls bit a splinter from the Last Load cart: with the wood still in her mouth, she then went secretly to a neighbour's house and crouched beneath the window to listen to the talk. The first male Christian name she overheard would be that of her future husband.

6

Farmers late with harvest mocked by their neighbours.

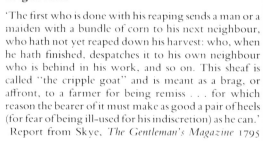

'The first who is done with his reaping sends a man or a maiden with a bundle of corn to his next neighbour, who hath not yet reaped down his harvest: who, when he hath finished, despatches it to his own neighbour who is behind in his work, and so on. This sheaf is called "the cripple goat" and is meant as a brag, or affront, to a farmer for being remiss . . . for which reason the bearer of it must make as good a pair of heels (for fear of being ill-used for his indiscretion) as he can.'
Report from Skye, *The Gentleman's Magazine* 1795

'If a Man or Woman shall have a Mole on the Over-brow, then let such a person refrain from Marriage altogether: for that such a person (if they marry) shall have five wives or five husbands in their life-time. And if a Man shall have a Mole in a manner behind the Neck, doth demonstrate that he shall be beheaded, except God (through earnest Prayer) prevent the same.'

The Shepherd's Prognostication 1729

September

Harvest-home dinners – variously called 'horkeys', 'mell-suppers', 'kern-feasts' and 'clyacks' – now being held everywhere.

7

In harvest time, harvest folk, servants and all
Should make, all together, good cheer in thy hall
Once ended thy harvest, let none be beguiled
Please such as did help thee, man, woman and child.
  Tusser *Five Hundred Points of Good Husbandry* 1573

'To make a rich frumenty for ten persons. Steep one pound of whole grains of wheat in water overnight, and then boil the steeped grains in one pint of milk until the whole be soft. Add thereto raisins and sultanas, honey, a nutmeg freshly grated, a little cinnamon, brandy and cream: and serve it forth hot or cold.'
  Mistress Barton's Cookery Book, *c.* 1680

The Feast of the Nativity of the Blessed Virgin Mary: more harvest-end fairs held, and harvest dinners continue.

8

The ceremony of drinking healths takes place in a sort of glee or catch:

  Here's a health unto our master
  He's the finder of the feast
  God bless his endeavours
  And send him increase
  And send him increase, boys
  All in another year.
    So drink, boys, drink
    And see you do not spill
    For if you do, you shall drink two
    For 'tis your master's will.
  Harvest in Norfolk: Hone's *Every Day Book* 1826

'For one that is or will be drunken. Take swallows and burn them, and make a powder of them; and give the man to drink thereof, and he shall never be drunk hereafter.'
  Edward Potter's Phisicke Book, 1610

9

Hedgerow trees and bushes beginning to fruit in most years.

A heavy crop of berries – and especially of hips and haws and of rowan berries – presages a hard winter: 'Many haws, many snows.'

> Rowan tree and red thread
> Hold the witches all in dread.

The many-titled rowan – alias mountain ash, quickbeam, wicken, witchbeam and witty – is the most powerful of all plants against evil and witchcraft. Hung above the door or planted in the garden, it protects house, family and beasts against spells; and rowan-wood walking sticks, whipstocks, yoke-pins or milk-churn staffs are all sovereign against the influence of witches and fairies: while rowan-wood in coffins prevents the dead from walking. Dry the orange-red berries and keep one in your pocket: or make them into a tangy jelly to eat with hare and rich meats.

10

Season of harvest-end festivals drawing to a close in southern Britain.

I've bin to Plymouth and I've bin to Dover
I've bin a-rambling, boys, all the world over
    Over and over and over and over
Drink up your liquor and turn yur cup over
    Over and over and over and over
The liquor's drink'd up and the cup is turned over.

For a popular Sussex harvest-dinner game, a cup of beer was placed on the flat crown of a top hat. Holding this by the brim with both hands, the player had to raise the cup to his lips and drink the contents before the fourth line of the song: and thereafter he had to flick the cup up, reverse the hat, and catch the cup in it. If he failed, or spilt any beer, he had to try again.

This was considered to be an especially fortunate day for the Parliamentary armies during the Civil War. On September the tenth 1643 they relieved Gloucester; on that day in 1645 they took Bristol; and on September the tenth 1649 Cromwell stormed Drogheda.

Hop-picking now beginning in Kent, Sussex and Herefordshire.

'What time your hops begin to change colour, somewhat before Michaelmas . . . you must gather them, and for the speedier despatch thereof procure as much help as you can, taking advantage of fair weather: and note that you were better to gather them too early than too late.'
Reginald Scott *The Perfite Platforme of a Hoppe Garden*
1574

Haste, haste then and strip, as it bends from the pole
The fruit that gives vigour and strength to the soul
Our hearts and our spirits to cheer
It warms and enlivens the true British beer.
Charles Dibdin *Songs* 1798

This season considered a good and effectual time to take medicine.

'Good for the heart: Saffron, borage, laughing, joy, musk, cloves, galingale, nutmegs, the red rose, the violet, mace.
'Evil for the heart: Beans, peas, leeks, garlic, onions, heaviness, anger, dread, too much business, travel, to drink cold water after labour, evil tidings.'
Kalendar of Shepheardes 1604

'Old Mr Rod near Hereford died since the coming in of Charles II, being then 106 years old. His diet was strange. He never ate flesh, nor fish, nor milk, nor butter, nor cheese; only hard eggs. But at 50 years old he ate the forehead of a roasted pig, and afterwards could eat any part of a pig; else, he never ate any flesh. He loved sack, but drank it temperately.'
John Aubrey *Observations c.* 1685

13

Hop-picking in full swing: Londoners, gypsies and itinerant workers flock into Kent.

> See, from the great metropolis they rush,
> The industrious vulgar! They, like prudent bees
> In Kent's wide garden road, expert to crop
> The flowery hop, and provident to work
> Ere winter numb their sunburnt hands.
>
> Christopher Smart *The Hop Garden* 1752

'The manifold virtues of Hops do manifestly argue the wholesomeness of beer above ale: for the hops rather make it a physical drink to keep the body in health, than an ordinary drink for the quenching of our thirst.'

Gerard's *Herbal* 1636

'In cleansing of blood hops help to cure the French diseases or pox, and all manner of scabs, itch . . . tetters, ringworm and spreading sores, the morphew and all discolouring of the skin. Half a dram of the seed taken in drink kills worms in the body.'

Culpeper's *Herbal* 1653

14

Holy Cross or Holy Rood Day: beginning of the nutting season.

Also called the Devil's Nutting Day, or the Day of the Holy Nut. The hazel-nuts (alias cob-nuts or filberts) collected today have magic properties. Look especially for double nuts, two on one stalk, which ward off rheumatism, toothache and the spells of witches. But beware that you do not pick them too early: for the hazel is a powerful tree, whose wood is used for divining rods, and to gather its nuts unripe is unlucky or even dangerous.

'For nuts, you shall know they are ripe as soon as you perceive them a little brown within the husk, or as it were ready to fall out of the same. After they be gathered, you shall shale them and take them clean out of their husks: then, for preserving them from either worms or dryness, it shall be good to lay them in some low cellar, where you cover them with sand, being first put into great bags or bladders.'

Markham *The English Husbandman* 1635

Nutting continues: begin fattening fowls for Michaelmas feasts.

15

'As a caution to persons at this season, when nuts are so very abundant, we state that the sudden death of Mr Nunn of Cley, Norfolk, is generally attributed to eating a great quantity of filberts and drinking port wine therewith.'

York Courant September 1794

'To fatten young Chicken in a wonderful degree: Boil rice in milk till it be very tender and pulpy. It must be thick, almost so thick that a spoon may stand on end in it. Sweeten this very well with ordinary sugar. Put this into their troughs where they feed, that they may always be eating of it. It must be made fresh every day, and their drink must be only milk, in another little trough. Let a candle (fitly disposed) stand by them all night, for seeing their food, and they will eat all night long.'

The Closet of Sir Kenelm Digby Opened 1669

St Ninian's Day: apples beginning to ripen.

16

St Ninian or Ringan (d.432) was a Romano-British bishop. Much venerated in Scotland, his shrine at Whithorn was a famous pilgrimage centre, and pilgrims still visit his cave on the sea-shore nearby.

Ninian's plant symbol is the herb southernwood, called 'apple-ringie' in Scotland and pressed in bibles to perfume them. Held by the Romans to be sovereign against spells causing impotence, under its English name of 'Lad's Love' it was presented by bachelors to the girl of their choice.

'Boiled with barley meal and laid unto them, southernwood takes away pimples, pushes or wheals that arise in the face, or other parts of the body.'

Culpeper's *Herbal* 1653

17

Fear strong winds, which shake unripe apples from the trees.

> September blow soft
> Until the apples be in the loft.

'As touching your Fallings, which are those Apples which fall from your trees, either through too much ripeness or else through the violence of wind, you shall by no means mix or match them with your gathered apples: for these Fallings must necessarily shrink, wither and grow rivelled the sooner, so that your best course is to spend them presently, with all speed possible.'

Markham *The English Husbandman* 1635

'The Hedge-hog commonly hath two holes or vents in his Den or Cave, the one towards the South, the other towards the North: look at which of them he stops, thence will great storms and winds follow.'

The Shepherd's Prognostication 1729

18

Avoid eating unripe fruit: and gather nettle seed, now abundant, to cure its ill effects.

> Green fruits make sickness to abound
> Use good advice to keep thee sound
> Give not thy lusts what they do crave
> Lest thou unwares step into grave.

Ranger's *Almanack* 1627

> The nettles stink, yet they make recompense
> If your belly by the Colic pain endures
> Against the Colic, take Nettle-seed and Honey
> Is Physic, better none is had for money
> It breedeth sleep, stays vomit, flegms doth soften
> It helps him of the Gout that eats it often.

Allestree's *Almanack* 1627

'Isaac Power being cut in the leg with a nip-hook, bled near a hat-full. The bleeding was stopped with stinging nettles stamped and pounded, and so laid on the cut. He learnt this receit in the army.'

John Aubrey *Observations* c. 1685

Wheat now plentiful for bread-making: be careful what kind you eat.

19

'Bread made of wheat maketh a man fat, especially when the bread is made of new wheat. Meslin bread is made, half of wheat and half of rye, and there is also meslin made, half of rye and half of barley. Evil bakers will put wheat and barley together: bread made of these aforesaid corns may fill the gut, but it shall never do good to man, no more than bread made of beans or peasen will do. Hot bread is unwholesome to any man, for it doth lie in the stomach like a sponge: yet the smell of new bread is comfortable to the head and heart. Old or stale bread doth dry up the blood or natural moisture in man and doth engender ill humours, and is evil and tardy of digestion: wherefore is no surfeit so evil as the surfeit of eating naughty bread.'

Andrew Boorde *Dietary of Health* 1547

Observe the weather: make lavender caps against the onset of winter.

20

The weather on the 20th, 21st and 22nd of September foretells the weather during the coming October, November and December respectively. If there is a south wind on these three days, for example, the succeeding months will be fair: but if they are wet the early winter will be gloomy.

'I judge that the flowers of lavender, quilted into a cap and daily worn, are good for all diseases of the head that come of a cold cause, and that they comfort the brain very well, namely if it have any distemperature that cometh of moistness.'

William Turner *Herbal* 1568.

21

St Matthew's Day: darker evenings and cooler weather now beginning.

> St Matthew, get candle new
> St Matthew
> Brings the cold rain and dew
> but   Matthew's Day bright and clear
> Brings good wine in next year.

St Matthew, Apostle and writer of the first Gospel, was a 'publican' or tax-gatherer before his conversion: he is therefore the patron saint of bankers, tax-collectors and others connected with finance.

'An excellent remedy for corns. Take black soap and snails, of each a like quantity, and stamp them together: spread it on a leather and lay it upon the corns. Put on a fresh plaster every fourth day.'

Doctor Lilly's Last Legacy 1683

22

Apples now ready to pick in most years.

'If you would have fruits to keep long, then let them not be over-ripe on the tree: and gather them about the first or last quarters of the moon.'

Lake's *Almanack* 1628

> The moon in the wane, gather fruit for to last
> But winter fruit gather, when Michael is past
> Though scrumpers that love not to buy or to crave
> Make some gather sooner – or else few to have.

Tusser *Five Hundred Points of Good Husbandry* 1573

'Such apples you would have take all possible leisure in ripening, those you shall lay neither upon fern nor straw, but upon the bare boards: nay, if you lay them upon a plaster floor (which is of all floors the coldest) till St Andrews-tide, it is not amiss, but very profitable, and the thinner you lay them, so much the better.'

Markham *The English Husbandman* 1635

SEPTEMBER

Hop-picking drawing to a close: cut bracken (or 'brakes') for winter fuel and cattle-litter.

23

End of hopping celebrations included 'harvest-suppers', and the ritual of plunging young couples (or farm bailiffs) into hop bins.

> The exulting band
> Of pickers, male and female, seize the fair
> Reluctant, and with boist'rous force and brute
> By cries unmoved, they bury her i' the bin
> Nor does the youth escape – him too they seize
> And in such posture place as best may serve
> To hide his charmer's blushes . . .
> Christopher Smart *The Hop Garden* 1752

Get home with thy brakes, ere all summer be gone
For tethered-up cattle to lie down upon.
Tusser *Five Hundred Points of Good Husbandry* 1573

Sun enters the House of Libra.

24

'The man born under Libra shall be right mightily praised and honoured in the service of Captains. He shall go in unknown places. He shall keep well his own, if he make not revelation in drink. He will not keep his promise. He will be married, but go from his wife. He shall be enriched by women, but experience evil fortune, though many shall ask counsel of him. He shall live 70 years after nature.

'The woman shall be amiable and of great courage, and shall go in places unknown. She shall be debonair and merry, rejoiced by her husband. If she be not wedded at 13, she shall not be chaste. After 30 years old she shall prosper the better and have great praise. She shall live 60 years after nature.'
Kalendar of Shepheardes 1604

25

Blackberries now ripe in hedges: pick them soon, before the Devil fouls them.

In Scotland, the Devil poisons the brambles on Old Holy Rood Day (September the 26th).

> Oh weans! Oh weans! the morn's the Fair
> Ye may na eat the berries mair
> This nicht the Deil gangs ower them a'
> To touch them with his pooshioned paw.

But in most of England he does not spit (or urinate) on them until Michaelmas: and some say he keeps to the old calendar, so that blackberries are safe to eat until Old Michaelmas (October the 10th).

'To cure the chin-cough or whooping cough. Creep under a Bramble that roots again in the ground at the other end.'

John Aubrey *Remains of Gentilism* 1688

'The leaves of the Bramble boiled in water, with honey, alum and a little white wine added thereto, make a most excellent lotion or washing water, and the same decoction fasteneth the teeth.'

Gerard *Herbal* 1636

26

Holy Rood Day, Old Style: known as Mid-Autumn Day in Highland Scotland, and traditionally the beginning of the mating season for deer.

'If the hart and hind meet dry and part dry on Holyrood Day, there will be no more rain for six weeks.' Whatever the weather is like in Scotland today, so it will continue for forty days hereafter.

In the Hebrides, women and girls ceremonially gathered St Michael's wild carrots at this time. The roots had to be taken in a particular way, by digging a triangular hole (signifying St Michael's shield) with a three-pronged mattock (St Michael's trident). Tied into bunches with a triple red thread, the carrots were presented to male visitors on Michaelmas Day: forked roots were especially lucky.

> Cleft, fruitful, fruitful, fruitful
> Joy of carrots surpassing upon me
> Michael the brave endowing me
> Bride the fair be aiding me

Carmina Gadelica

The Feast of Saints Cosmas and Damian: lay in supplies for the Michaelmas dinner.

27

Saints Cosmas and Damian, 'the holy moneyless ones', were two Christian doctors from Syria who practised medicine without charging fees, but were martyred for their faith. They are therefore the patrons of doctors, apothecaries and barbers, and are invoked against hernia and pestilence.

Michaelmas Daisies now in bloom. The purple garden flower (which has escaped into the countryside) was introduced from New England in the 1640s: but the native blue-purple sea aster and the white feverfew are also called 'michaelmas daisies' in some counties.

The Eve of Michaelmas: preparations being made everywhere for tomorrow's celebration.

28

In the Scottish Highlands and Islands, the Michaelmas Lamb – a ram lamb without blemish – was killed today, and the Struan Michael or Michaelmas Cake prepared. This was made from equal parts of all the types of grain grown on the farm, kneaded with butter, eggs and sheep's milk: it was then marked with a cross and cooked on a stone heated by a fire of sacred oak, rowan and bramble-wood. Sometimes a piece of struan might be thrown into the fire, as a 'tithe' to placate St Michael's old opponent the Devil.

In Surrey, Michaelmas Eve was Crack-Nut Day, when nuts were cracked and eaten in churches: while in Yorkshire and Lincolnshire bonfires were lit, and grain was scattered for the wild birds, to bring luck to the farm. There, too, a watcher who dared wait in the church porch at midnight would see the spirits of those parishioners destined to die in the following year.

29 Michaelmas, the feast of St Michael the Archangel and the greatest of the autumn festivals.

Michael the Archangel, Captain of the Host of Heaven, fought against Satan and his evil angels and cast them out of Paradise (*Revelations* XII 7–9). He is thus the patron of knights and warriors, and of the high places (like St Michael's Mount in Cornwall) whose churches are often dedicated to him. He is also the guardian of the souls of the dead, whose good and bad deeds he weighs in his scales.

'If you eat roast goose on Michaelmas Day, you will never want money all the year.'

'Sauce for a stubble goose: Take the pap of roasted apples, and mixing it with Vinegar, boil them together on the fire with some of the gravy of the goose and a few Barberries and bread crumbs: when it is boiled to a good thickness, season it with sugar and a little cinnamon, and so serve it forth.'

Markham *The English Housewife* 1683

30 Michaelmas Hiring Fairs now being held: finish off Michaelmas goose.

In southern Britain, this was the time of 'hirings', 'mops', or 'stattis', when young unmarried labourers and servants flocked to fairs to hire themselves out for the year, bargaining with masters for the best possible wage.

The master that a servant wants will now stand in a
wonder
You all must ask ten pounds a year, and none of you go
under
It's you must do all the work, and what they do
require
So stand up for your wages, lads, before that you do
hire.
Hiring broadside ballad, Yorkshire

Examine the breast-bone of the goose by holding it up to the light. If it is dark, a hard winter is coming; if mottled, a variable one; and if almost transparent, a mild winter. The colour of the front part of the bone foreshows the early winter: its back half the winter after Christmas.

OCTOBER

FRUIT-TIME AND FALL-OF-LEAF

The eighth month of the Roman calendar.
In Welsh: *Hydref* – the month of autumn.
In Gaelic: *An Damhair* – the month of deer rutting.
In Anglo-Saxon: *Wintirfyllith* – the month of the winter moon.

1

October hath always: one and twenty fine days.

If the October moon comes without frost, expect no frost till the full moon of November.

> This month hot drinks and meals be good
> To keep thy health and nourish thy blood
> Provide warm clothes, and go foot-dry
> Thou shalt escape much danger thereby.
>
> Neve's *Almanack* 1633

> In October, dung your field
> And all your land its wealth will yield.

2

The proper time of the year to make sympathetic or magnetic potions to cure wounds: these were applied to the weapon which caused the wound, instead of to the wound itself.

'A medicine to cure by the weapon: published by Rodolphus Goclorus Professor of Physic in Wittenberg in the year 1608 and entitled the magnetical cure. Take of the moss on the skull of a strangled man two ounces; of the mummia of man's blood an ounce and a half; of earthworms washed in water or wine an ounce and a half; of the hemetitis two ounces; of the fat of a boar and a boar pig, two drams each; oil of turpentine two drams. Pound them and keep them in a narrow pot, and make this cure when the sun is in Libra. Dip into the ointment the iron or wood of the weapon, or if the weapon cannot be had a sallow stick made wet with blood in opening the wound. And let the patient wash his wound in the morning with his own urine and bind it with a clean cloth, always wiping away the matter.'

Fairfax Household Book, 17th/18th century

Gather apples to sweat for cider-making.

3

'If the Apples are made up immediately from the Tree, they are observed to yield more, but not so good Cider as when hoarded the space of a month, or a fortnight at the least . . . and if the apples be shakened down before their time by a Violent wind, it is observed to be so indispensably necessary that they lie together in hoard, at least till the usual time of their maturity, that the Cider otherwise is seldom or never found worthy the drinking.'

John Newburgh *Observations on Cider* 1678

'If you gather not by hand (which is Tedious) Lay a truss of Straw beneath the Tree and over that a blanket, discreetly shaking them down, not too many at a time, but often carrying them where they are to sweat: which should be on dry boarded floors, by no means on earth unless Straw lie under. By ten or fourteen days they will have done sweating: but the greener they are when gathered, let them lie the longer.'

Cook *The Making of Cider* 1678

St Francis's Day: swallows preparing to migrate.

4

The disappearance of swallows and other migrants in the autumn was for long a great mystery. Some firmly believed that they hibernated at the bottom of lakes or ponds, and others that they hid in holes and bushes and remained torpid until spring.

'In the northern waters, fishermen oftentimes by chance draw up in their nets an abundance of Swallows, hanging together like a conglomerated mass. In the beginning of Autumn, they assemble themselves together among the reeds by ponds, where, allowing themselves to sink into the water, they join bill to bill, wing to wing and foot to foot.'

Olaus Magnus *History of the Northern Nations* 1550

'But if hirundines hide in rocks and caverns, how do they, while torpid, avoid being eaten by weasels and other vermin?'

Gilbert White *Naturalist's Journal* 1776

5 Seek out oak-apples and observe their condition.

'If thou wilt see and know how it will go that year, then take heed of the Oak-Apples about St Michael's Day. When they be within full of Spiders, then followeth a naughty Year; if they have with them Flies, that betokens a good Year, or if they have Maggots in them; if there be nothing in them, then followeth a great Dearth. If they be many, and early ripe, so shall it be an early Winter, and much Snow afore Christmas, and after that much cold: if the inner Part be fair and clear, then shall the Summer be fair and the corn good; but if they be very moist, then shall the Summer also be moist.'

The Knowledge of Things Unknown 1729

6 St Faith's Day: season of corn sowing.

St Faith or Foi, a virgin martyr, is said to have been executed by being grilled over a fire. Cakes were therefore made in her honour, and in northern England these were used by young girls to divine the identity of their future husbands.

On St Faith's evening, three girls should join in making a cake of flour, salt, sugar and spring water: this should be turned nine times as it bakes, each girl turning it thrice. Then it should be cut in three, each girl's share being divided again into nine slivers: and every sliver must be passed thrice through a wedding ring belonging to a woman married seven years at least. All the slivers are then eaten, while repeating:

> O good St Faith, be kind tonight
> And bring to me my heart's delight
> Let me my future husband view
> And be my vision chaste and true.

After hanging the ring from their bed-head on a cord, the girls must then go straight to bed: and they will dream of their husbands-to-be.

Gather damsons and plums before the frost attacks them.

'To preserve Damsons. Take Damsons before they be full ripe, but gathered off the Tree. Allow to every pound of them a pound of Sugar, put a little Rose-water to them, and set them in the bottom of your pan one by one. Boil them with a soft fire, and as they seeth strew your Sugar upon them, and let them boil till the Syrup be thick. Then while the Syrup is yet warm, take the Damsons out and put them into a covered gally pot, Syrup and all.'

Thomas Jenner *A Book of Fruits and Flowers* 1653

'All Plums are under Venus, and are like women, some better and some worse. As there is a great diversity of kinds, so there is in the operation of Plums, for some that are sweet moisten the stomach, and make the belly soluble: those that are sour quench thirst more, and bind the belly. The moist and waterish do sooner corrupt in the stomach, but the firm do nourish more, and offend less.'

Culpeper *Herbal* 1653

'Avoid being out late at Nights, or in foggy Weather: for a Cold now got, may continue the whole Winter.'

The Court and City Register 1759

'The Autumn dry and full of cold north Winds doth greatly vex those of a melancholy complexion with daily Agues and other Diseases: but is good for women and such phlegmatique creatures. Very cold and moist Autumn breeds coughs, stoppings, headaches and the like.'

Dove's *Almanack* 1627

'For an Ague. Take clean Spiderweb half a dram and swallow it down in any form for several mornings successively. When the fit is off, take six drams of bark, a spoonful of pepper and a nutmeg mixed up with rum or wine. Take of this about the bigness of a nut every four hours. It is proved.'

Fairfax Household Book, 17th/18th century

9

St Denis's Day: loose pigs to fatten on fallen beech-mast and acorns, but ring their noses to prevent them rooting up pasture land.

> October good blast
> To blow the hog mast.

To gather some mast, it shall stand thee upon
With servant and children, ere mast all be gone
Some left among bushes shall pleasure thy swine
For fear of a mischief keep acorns from kine
For rooting of pasture ring hog ye had need
Which being well ringled the better doth feed.
Tusser *Five Hundred Points of Good Husbandry* 1573

'In Herefordshire the chamber-pots are emptied into the hogwash; and it is asserted that the usage of pigs to food with this mixture occasions them to refuse no kind of sustenance, possibly because nothing can be worse.'

The Gentleman's Magazine 1819

10

Old Michaelmas Day: often brings a spell of fine weather, called 'Michaelmas Spring'.

Flocks of migrating geese seen passing over: Old Michaelmas Goose Fairs and Hiring Fairs held about this time, notably at Nottingham.

'None have seen the Barnacle Goose's nest or egg; nor is this surprising, since such geese are said to have spontaneous generation in the following way. When the firwood masts or planks of ships have rotted in the sea, then a kind of fungus breaks out upon them: in which after a time the plain form of birds may be seen, and these become clothed in feathers, and eventually come to life and fly away as Barnacle Geese.'

William Turner *On Birds* 1544

Use up sweet eating apples to make water–cider.

11

'Doctor Harvey's pleasant Water-cider, whereof He used to drink much. Take one bushel of pippins, cut them into slices with the Peelings and Cores: boil them in twelve gallons of water, till the goodness of them be in the water, and that consumed about three gallons. Then strain it through a bag made of cotton: and when it is clear run out and almost cold, sweeten it with five pounds of Brown Sugar. Put a pint of Ale-yeast to it, and set it working two nights and days. Then skim off the yeast clean, and put it into bottles, and let it stand two or three days till the yeast fall dead at the top. Take this off clean with a knife, and fill it up a little within the neck (so that a finger's breadth be empty below the stopple) and then stop the bottles and tie them, or else it will drive out the Corks. Within a fortnight you may drink it: and it will keep five or six weeks.'

The Closet of Sir Kenelm Digby Opened 1669

If the wind is in the west today, a mild winter will follow: make ready cider mills and presses.

12

'The best Mills to grind in, are those of Stone, which resemble a Millstone set edge-ways, moved round the Trough by an horse, till the Fruit be bruised small enough for the Press.'

Colwall *Account of Perry and Cider* 1678

Now prepare
Materials for thy Mill, a sturdy Post
Cylindric, to support the Grinder's Weight
Nor must thou not be mindful of thy Press
Long e'er the Vintage: but with timely Care
Shave the Goat's shaggy beard, lest thou too late
In vain shouldst seek a strainer
Be cautious next a Proper Steed to find
Whose prime is past: the vigorous Horse disdains
Such servile labours . . .
Blind Bayard rather, worn with work and years
Shall roll th' unwieldy stone with sober Pace.

John Philips *Cider* 1708

13

St Edward the Confessor's Day: seek cures for the King's Evil.

The Anglo-Saxon King Edward the Confessor (d.1065) was revered as a saint even in his own lifetime: and from him English monarchs derived their unique power of healing by a touch the painful and disfiguring throat sickness of scrofula, known therefore as the King's Evil.

English monarchs touched for the Evil until the time of Queen Anne, the most inveterate practitioner being Charles II, who laid hands on more than 92,000 sufferers between 1660 and 1682. The ceremony included the hanging about the patient's neck of a gold medallion: some accordingly believed that the gold performed the cure, others that patients applied for the cure in order to get the gold.

'To know whether a malady be the King's Evil. Take a ground worm alive and lay him upon the swelling or sore and cover him with a leaf. If it be the disease, the worm will turn to earth: but if it be not the Evil, he will remain whole and sound.'

Fairfax Household Book, 17th/18th century

14

As the days grow darker and Halloween approaches, beware of witches.

'John Greencliffe of Beverley sayeth that on Saturday last, about seven in the evening, Elizabeth Roberts did appear to him in her usual wearing clothes, with a ruff about her neck: and, presently vanishing, turned herself into the similitude of a cat, which fixed close about his leg and after much struggling vanished. Whereupon he was much pained at his heart. Upon Wednesday there seized a cat upon his body, which did strike him on the head, upon which he fell into a swound or trance. After he received the blow, he saw the said Elizabeth escape upon a wall in her usual wearing apparel. Upon Thursday she appeared in the likeness of a bee, which did very much afflict him: to wit, in throwing of his body from place to place, notwithstanding there were five or six persons to hold him down.'

York Castle Trial Records, October 1654

Sow acorns for timber in fenced plantations: gather quinces and store them to ripen.

15

Sow acorns ye owners, that timber doth love
Sow haws and rye with them the better to prove
If cattle or coney may enter to crop
Young oak is in danger of losing his top.
Tusser *Five Hundred Points of Good Husbandry* 1573

'Now for Quinces, they are a fruit which by no means you may place near any other kind of fruit, because their scent is so strong and piercing, that it will enter into any fruit and clean take away his natural relish. The time of their gathering is ever in October: and the meetest place to lie them in is where they may have most air and lie dry (for wet they can by no means endure): also they must not lie close, because the smell of them is both strong and unwholesome.'

Markham *The English Husbandman* 1635

Observe the ears.

16

'Significations from the Ears. The Ears long and narrow, denote a person to be envious; standing very near the head, to be dull and sluggish; the Ears hairy, to be a long liver, and quick of hearing. The Ears small, to be a scoffer; the Ears big, to be dull; the Ears hanging, to be a fool; the Ears over-round, to be unapt to learn: the Ears of a mean and proper bigness, to be faithful and honest-conditioned.'

The Shepherd's Prognostication 1729

If your ears burn or tingle, someone is talking of you: if the left ear, they speak harm; if the right, they speak well.

'For deafness: Take the gall of an hare and mix it with woman's milk. Put these into the ear warm and stop it close with black wool: it healeth in nine days.'

Fairfax Household Book, 17th/18th century

17

Beware of earthquakes.

'Near unto the place where Lugg and Wye meet together, eastward, a hill which they call Marcley-hill, in the year of our redemption 1571 (as though it had wakened from a deep sleep) roused itself up, and for the space of three days together moving and shoving itself (as mighty and huge an heap as it was) with roaring noise in a fearful sort, and overturning all things that stood in the way, advanced itself forward to the wondrous astonishment of the beholders.'

Camden *Britannia* 1695

I nor advise, nor reprehend the Choice
Of Marcley-hill; the Apple no where finds
A kinder Mold: Yet 'tis unsafe to trust
Deceitful Ground. Who knows but that, once more,
This Mount may journey and, his present Site
Forsaking, to thy Neighbours' Bounds transfer
Thy goodly Plants, affording Matter strange
For Law-debates.

John Philips *Cider* 1708

18

St Luke's Day: fine weather, called 'St Luke's Little Summer', to be expected about now in southern England.

St Luke, the Greek writer of the third Gospel and the Acts of the Apostles, is the patron saint both of doctors and of painters and other artists.

St Luke's is a lucky day to choose a husband.

To dream of your future husband. Before going to bed on St Luke's night, anoint your stomach, breast and lips with a powder of dried marigold flowers, marjoram, thyme and wormwood, simmered in virgin honey and white vinegar. Then repeat three times

St Luke, St Luke, be kind to me
In dreams let me my true love see.

During the night your future husband will appear, 'very plain and visible to be seen'. If he will prove a loving partner, he will smile at you: but if 'after marriage he will forsake thy bed to wander after strange women, he will offer to be rude and uncivil with thee'.

St Luke's-tide lovers exchange tokens and set the wedding date.

19

'It was anciently very customary . . . to break a piece of Gold or Silver in token of a verbal contract of marriage and promises of love; one half whereof was kept by the woman, while the other part remained with the man.'

Brand *Popular Antiquities* 1813

Marry in September's shine
Your living will be rich and fine
If in October you do marry
Love will come but riches tarry
If you wed in bleak November
Only joy will come, remember
When December's showers fall fast
Marry and true love will last.

Monday for wealth
Tuesday for health
Wednesday the best day of all
Thursday for crosses
Friday for losses
Saturday, no luck at all.

Inspect stores of sweating cider-apples.

20

'The old sorts of apple are the most valuable for cider, such as the Stire; Golden-pippin; Hagloe crab; several varieties of the Harvey; the Brady-apple; Red-streak; Woodcock; Moyle; Gennet-moyle; red, white and yellow Musks; Fox-whelp; Loan and Old Pearmains; Dymock-red; Ten Commandments and others.'

Herefordshire Orchards: A Pattern for England 1657

'A convenient quantity of rotten apples mixed with the sound is greatly assistant to the work of fermentation, and notably helps to clarify the cider. A friend of mine having made provision of apples for cider, whereof so great a part were found rotten when the time for grinding them came that they did (as it were) wash the room with their juice, had cider from them not only passable but exceeding good.'

John Newburgh *Observations on Cider* 1678

21

The feast of St Ursula and her Eleven Thousand Virgins: make the Virgin Queen's potion.

St Ursula ('little bear') is said to have been a British princess who fled with her maiden companions to avoid an unwanted marriage, but was martyred with them by the Huns at Cologne, whose cathedral was raised in their honour. The virgin band, whose number was expanded from eleven to eleven thousand by medieval fable, are the patrons of girls' schools.

'Queen Elizabeth her potion for Wind. Take ginger, cinnamon, galingale, of each one ounce; aniseeds, caraway seeds, fennel seeds, of each half an ounce; mace and nutmegs two drams each; pound all together and add one pound of white sugar. Use this powder after or before meat at any time. It comforteth the stomach, helpeth digestion, and expels wind greatly.'

Fairfax Household Book, 17th/18th century

22

By tradition, the anniversary of the Creation: timber felling begins.

'In the beginning God created Heaven and Earth. Which beginning of time, according to our Chronology, fell upon the entrance of the night preceding the twenty-third day of October, in the year 4004 before Christ.'

James Ussher *The Annals of the World* 1658

'One shrouding a tree in North Wales fell down on his head, and turning his brain, lay for dead. A mason, an ingenious fellow, advised he should have a strong coffin made, with his feet to come to one end, his head not to touch the other by two inches. Then with a huge axe he gave a sound knock at the feet, to turn by that contrary motion his brain right again. After the blow was given, the fellow groaned and spake, and recovered.'

John Aubrey *Observations c.* 1685

23

Leaves begin to fall from the trees: signs of winter increase.

'When the Leaves will not fall from the Trees in October, or else when there are a great number of Caterpillars on the Trees, then followeth after a cold Winter.'

The Knowledge of Things Unknown 1729

If the birds are fat in October, expect a hard winter.

Flocks of winter migrant woodcock arrive about now: they were once believed to spend summer on the Moon.

Some think to northern coasts their flight they tend
Or, to the moon in midnight hours ascend.

John Gay *The Shepherd's Week* 1714

Anniversary of the battle of Edgehill, 1642, the first major conflict of the Civil War: 'which was afterward divers several times observed to be acted by phantasms in the sky, with the clashing of weapons and piteous cries of the wounded, to the wonder and no small terror of the witnesses thereof.'

24

Sun enters the House of Scorpio.

'The man born under Scorpio shall have good fortune. He shall be a great fornicator, and the first wife he shall have in marriage shall become too religious. He shall suffer pain in his privy members at fifteen years old. He shall be hardy as a lion: he shall be merry, and love good company of merry folk. He shall be in danger of enemies at twenty-four years, and if he escape he shall live eighty-four years.

'The woman shall be amiable and fair: she will not be long with her first husband, and afterward shall enjoy with another by her good and true service. She shall suffer pain in her stomach and wounds in her shoulders, and ought to fear her latter days, which shall be doubtful by reason of venom. She shall live seventy years after nature.'

Kalendar of Shepheardes 1604

25

St Crispin and Crispinian's Day; Agincourt Day.

Crispin. Crispianus.

According to a highly dubious legend, Saints Crispin and Crispinian were brother shoemakers of Soissons in France (or some say of Faversham in Kent) who were martyred by being pricked to death with cobbler's awls. They are therefore the patrons of shoemakers, and their day is the cobbler's feast or 'Snobs' Holiday'.

> The twenty-fifth of October
> Cursed be the cobbler
> That goes to bed sober.

Anniversary of the great English victory at Agincourt, 1415.

> This day is called the Feast of Crispian . . .
> And Crispin Crispian shall ne'er go by
> From this day to the ending of the world
> But we in it shall be remembered.
> Shakespeare *Henry V* IV iii, 1599

26

Gather sloes for a sure remedy against diarrhoea: or to make sloe gin, wine, or jelly.

> By th' end of October, go gather up sloes
> Have thou in a readiness plenty of those
> And keep them in bedstraw, or still on the bough
> To stay both the flux of thyself and thy cow.
> Tusser *Five Hundred Points of Good Husbandry* 1573

'For the Lask or extreme scouring of thy belly, take the seeds of the Wood-rose or Briar-rose, beat it to powder, and mix a dram thereof with an ounce of the conserve of Sloes and eat it: it will in a short space bind and make the belly hard.'
> Markham *The English Housewife* 1683

Sloes for keeping are best taken not quite ripe, and stored still on the branch: but sloes for wine or jelly (wherein some mix them with apples to take away their sharpness) should be left until after they have weathered a sharp frost or two.

Begin cider-pressing.

'Being ground, let your bruised apples continue twenty-four hours before pressing: 'twill give your Cider the more Amber-bright colour, and hinder its over-fermenting.'

Cook *Cider-making* 1664

'This done, they put the fruit up into a Crib [and] put a stone on it, but first they fit a circle of fresh straw about the Crib, to preserve the bruised fruit from bursting through the Crib when they apply the Screws . . . which turn on a great Beam to crush the fruit down with the more force, by which means it is wrung so dry, as nothing can be had more out of it.'

Colwall *An Account of Perry and Cider* 1678

'The last running of the Cider, bottled immediately from the Press, is by some esteemed a pure and well-relished liquor: but in Devonshire, where their Wrings or Presses are so hugely great, that an Hogshead or two runs commonly out before the Apples suffer any considerable pressure, they value this first running above any other.'

John Newburgh *Observations on Cider* 1678

St Simon and St Jude's Day: expect rain.

Saints Simon and Jude were among Christ's Twelve Apostles, and some say that they were the shepherds to whom the angels announced Jesus's birth. Simon, traditionally martyred by being sawn in half, is the patron of woodcutters, but it is not clear why Jude is the saint of lost causes, invoked by those in desperate straits.

It is certain to rain heavily on the day of Simon and Jude.

On this day, carefully peel an apple in one long strip: and turn round thrice with the peel in your right hand, repeating

> St Simon and Jude, on you I intrude
> By this paring I hold to discover
> Without any delay, to tell me this day
> The first letter of my own true lover.

Then drop the peel over your left shoulder, and it will form the initial of your future spouse's surname: but if it instead breaks in many pieces, you will probably never marry.

29

Warden pears now in season: borrow a spayed bitch against Halloween.

'To stew wardens or pears. Peel them, put them into a Pipkin, with so much Red or Claret-wine and water as will near reach to the top of the Pears. Stew or boil gently, till they grow tender, which may be in two hours. After a while, put in some sticks of Cinnamon bruised and a few Cloves. When they are almost done, put in Sugar enough to season them well and their Syrup, which you pour out upon them in a deep plate.'
The Closet of Sir Kenelm Digby Opened 1669

'I believe all over England, a Spayed Bitch is accounted wholesome in a House: that is to say, they have a strong belief that it keeps away evil spirits from haunting of a House . . . at Cranborn in Dorset about 1686, a House was haunted, and two Tenants successively went away for that reason: a third came and brought his spayed bitch, and was never troubled.'
John Aubrey *Remains of Gentilism* 1688

30

Make preparations for Halloween.

'Certainly, some one knave in a white sheet hath cozened and abused many thousands . . . for in our childhood our mother's maids have so terrified us with an ugly devil having horns on his head, fire in his mouth and a tail in his breech, eyes like a basin, fangs like a dog and a voice roaring like a lion, whereby we start and are afraid when we hear one cry 'Bough' . . . in so much as some never fear the devil, but in a dark night: and then a polled sheep is a perilous beast, and many times is taken for our father's soul, especially in a churchyard, where a right hardy man heretofore scant durst pass by night, but his hair would stand upright.'
Reginald Scot *The Discovery of Witchcraft* 1584

OCTOBER

Halloween or All Hallows E'en: the eve of All Saints Day and of Samhain, also called Winter's Eve: the last night of the Celtic year and the uncanniest season in the whole calendar.

31

The Night of the Dead, when the ghosts of the departed revisit the earth and witches and evil spirits wield their greatest power. The Fairy Court rides out at midnight, and only at this precise moment may those kidnapped by the Good Folk be saved by their lovers.

> Just at the mirk and midnight hour
> The Fair Folk will ride
> They that would their true love win
> At Miles Cross they must bide.
>
> The Ballad of Tam Lin

> Hey how for Hallow E'en
> A' the witches tae be seen
> Some in black and some in green
> Hey how for Hallow E'en
>
> Scots rhyme

Bonfires should be lit on hilltops to drive off witches: and on no account let the household fire go out tonight, or evil things may gain an entry.

With the Unseen now pressing so close to mankind, this is the best night of the year to divine the identity of your future husband or wife.

Take a candle and go alone to a mirror in a darkened room: eat an apple while looking into it, combing your hair all the while: and the face of your lover – or of the Devil – will appear over your shoulder.

For each couple, place a pair of nuts, corn grains or apple pips near the fire or on a hot shovel: in Wales, if both 'pop and fly' simultaneously, the couple will marry, but if they explode at different times they will part. In Scotland and northern England, the nuts should burn quietly together, and if they spring apart, so will the couple: but in the south they say

> If he loves me, pop and fly
> If he hates me, lie and die.

NOVEMBER

THE MONTH OF BLOOD AND BONFIRES

The ninth month of the Roman calendar.
In Welsh: *Tachwedd* – the month of slaughtering; or *Y Mis Du* – the black month.
In Gaelic: *An t-Samhuinn* – the month of the Samhain festival.
In Anglo–Saxon: *Blotmonath* – the month of blood.

NOVEMBER

The Feast of All Saints or All Hallows: which is also Samhain, the pagan Celtic New Year festival when stored fruits and crops were blessed and the dead were remembered.

1

'All the gods of this world were worshipped on this day, from sunrise to sunset.'

Irish saying

On All Saints night, 'soul-cakes' were made and distributed to the poor, who prayed in return for the souls of the departed: and the returning dead were thought somehow to share in the cakes.

A child born at Hallowtide is sure to have the Second Sight, and all November's children will be fortunate and beloved.

> November's child is born to bless
> He's like a song of thankfullness.

'When All Saints comes on a Wednesday, the men of all the earth will be under affliction.'

Highland proverb

All Souls Day or Soulmass, when the Dead are especially prayed for.

2

'Tindle' bonfires burnt to light souls out of Purgatory: soul-caking continues, and today a cake should be given to every visitor to the house.

'In the County of Hereford was an old Custom at Funerals, to hire poor people, who were to take upon them all the Sins of the party deceased. One of them I remember (he was a long, lean, lamentable poor rascal). The manner was that when a Corpse was brought out of the house and laid on the Bier; a Loaf of bread was brought out and delivered to the Sin-eater over the corps, as also a Mazer-bowl full of beer, which he was to drink up, and sixpence in money, in consideration whereof he took upon him all the Sins of the Defunct, and freed him (or her) from Walking after they were dead.'

John Aubrey *Remains of Gentilism* 1688

3

Icy weather now presages a mild Christmas, and vice-versa: doctor chilblains as soon as they appear.

> If ducks do slide at Hallowentide
> At Christmas they will swim
> If ducks do swim at Hallowentide
> At Christmas they will slide.

'To know whether the Winter shall be cold or warm, go at Allhallows-tide to a Beech tree, and cut a chip thereof: if it be found Dry, then shall the Winter be warm.'

The Shepherd's Prognostication 1729

'For Chilblains and Kibes. Take fair water and wheat-bran, and seeth it till it be very soft, and lay it upon the place grieved so hot as you can suffer it: if the chilblain be broken it will heal it, and if it be not broken it will assuage it.'

Fairfax Household Book, 17th/18th century

4

Collect wood for Guy Fawkes bonfire: make gingerbread and 'Plot toffee'.

> A stick and a stake
> For King George's sake
> Will you please to give us a faggot
> If you won't give one, we'll steal two
> The better for we and the worse for you.

Warwickshire rhyme

'To make Gingerbread: Take Claret-wine, and put in sugar, and set it to the fire; then take wheat bread finely grated and sifted, and Liquorice, Anniseeds, Ginger and Cinnamon beaten very small into powder. Mix your bread and your spice together, put them into the wine, and boil it, and stir it until it be very thick. Then mould it and print it at your pleasure, and let it stand in a place neither too moist nor too warm.'

Markham *The English Housewife* 1683

Guy Fawkes Night, or Gunpowder Treason Day.

5

'We yield thee our unfeigned thanks and praise, for the wonderful and mighty deliverance of our late gracious sovereign King James the First . . . with the Nobility, Clergy and Commons of this Realm then assembled in Parliament, by Popish Treachery appointed as sheep to the slaughter in a most barbarous and savage manner . . .'

The Form of Prayer with Thanksgiving to be used upon the Fifth Day of November, in the *Book of Common Prayer*

'Sir Thomas Knevet, searching the cellar . . . first found one of the small Barrels of Powder, and after all the rest, to the number of thirty-six Barrels. And thereafter searching the fellow (Faux) whom he had taken, found ready upon him three matches and all other instruments fit for blowing up the powder . . . whereby King and Parliament should have been all destroyed and blown up at once.'

A Discourse on the Late Intended Treason 1605

Please to remember the fifth of November
The gunpowder treason and plot
I see no reason why gunpowder treason
Should ever be forgot
'Twas God's mercy to be sent
To save our King and Parliament
Three score barrels laid below, for old England's overthrow
With a lighted candle, with a lighted match
Boom, boom, to let him in.

Hertfordshire rhyme

Begin threshing corn: look out for the winter constellation Orion.

6

'The wintry and huge constellation, Orion, begins now to make his appearance in the evening, exhibiting his enormous figure in the east.'

Gilbert White *Naturalist's Journal* 1781

'When the Stars be misty and dark, as though they shined through a mist, though there be no Clouds in the Element, it is a Token of Trouble in the Air, and much Rain and Snow.'

The Knowledge of Things Unknown 1729

7

Attempt the cure of persons acting strangely after Halloween.

'A remedy for those bewitched. Take two horseshoes, heat them red hot, and nail one on the threshold of the door, but Quench the other in the Urine of the party bewitched: then set the urine over the fire in a pot or pipkin, and put the horseshoe into it. Make the urine boil, with a little salt put unto it, and three horseshoe nails, until it is almost all consumed: what is not boiled away, cast into the fire. Keep then your horseshoes and nails in a clean paper or cloth, and use the same manner three times. It will be the more effectual if it be done at the change or full of the Moon.'

Doctor Lilly's Last Legacy 1683

'The fables of Witchcraft have taken so fast hold and deep rooted in the heart of man, that if any adversity, grief, sickness, loss of children, corn, cattle or liberty happen unto them, by and by they exclaim upon witches.'

Reginald Scot *The Discovery of Witchcraft* 1584

8

Complete cider-pressing: make cider-syllabub.

Some, when the Press, by utmost Vigour screwed
Has drained the pulpous Mass, regale their Swine
With the dry Refuse: thou more wise shalt steep
Thy Husks in Water, and again employ
The ponderous Engine. Water will imbibe
The small remains of Spirit, and acquire
A vinous Flavour: this the Peasants blithe
With quaff, and whistle, as thy tinkling Team
They drive . . .

John Philips *Cider* 1708

'To make an excellent Cyder-Syllabub. Fill your pot with Cyder and good store of Sugar and a little Nutmeg: stir it well together, and put in as much thick Cream as you put Cyder, by two or three spoonfulls at a time. Then stir all exceedingly softly but once about, and let it stand two hours at least ere it is eaten, for the standing makes the curd.'

The Compleat Cook 1671

Complete the fattening of pigs for Martinmas slaughter.

'The best feeding of a Swine for Lard or a Boar for Brawn, is to feed them the first week with Barley sodden till it break; then after to feed them with raw malt from the floor, before it be dried, till they be fat enough: then for a week after to give them dry Pease or Beans to harden their flesh. Let their drink be the washings of Ale-barrels and Sweet Whey. This manner of feeding breeds the whitest, fattest and best flesh that may be, as hath been approved by the best Husbands.'

Markham *Cheap and Good Husbandry* 1683

'Make your pig quite fat by all means. The last bushel, even if he sit as he eat, is the most profitable. If he can walk two hundred yards at a time, he is not well fatted. Lean bacon is the most wasteful thing that any family can use. . . . The man that cannot live on solid fat bacon . . . wants the sweet sauce of labour, or is fit for the hospital.'

William Cobbett *Cottage Economy* 1822

Martinmas Eve, which is Halloween Old Style and thus a second chance to look into the future.

The trial of the three dishes, as performed in Scotland. Take three dishes, fill one with clean and another with dirty water, and leave one empty. The person making the trial is then blindfolded and led in, to feel for a dish with their left hand: if they put their hand into the clean water, their future wife (or husband) will be a maid or bachelor; if into the dirty, they will wed a widow or widower; but if into the empty dish, they will never marry. The trial should be repeated three times, changing the arrangement of the dishes between each attempt.

Unusually hard weather now presages a mild winter.

If Martinmas ice will bear a duck
Then look for a winter of slush and muck.

But a spell of fine weather, 'St Martin's Little Summer', is more usual now.

11

Martinmas: the festival of winter's beginning, of blood-letting and fresh meat.

St Martin of Tours (d.397) was a young Roman cavalry officer, who was moved by charity to divide his cloak with a beggar, subsequently revealed as Christ Himself. He is thus the patron of soldiers, beggars and the oppressed.

With grazing now becoming scanty, Martinmas was the traditional time for slaughtering all cattle, sheep and pigs which could not be maintained through the winter. It was therefore an unusual and welcome opportunity for feasting on fresh meat.

> It is the day of Martinmas
> Cups of ale should freely pass
> What though winter has begun
> To push down the summer sun
> To our fire we can betake
> And enjoy the crackling brake
> Never heeding winter's face
> On the day of Martinmas.

12

Cure meat for winter stores: make puddings and sausages from offal.

> Martinmas Beef doth bear good tack
> When country folk do dainties lack,

A whole cow or sheep, now either salted or set in the chimney to dry-cure like bacon, often provided the only winter meat supply for many less prosperous families. Its innards, meanwhile, provided puddings and sausages.

'To make Excellent Black-puddings. Take a quart of Sheeps-blood or Pigs-blood warm, and a quart of Cream: ten Eggs, the yolks and whites beaten well together. Stir all this liquor very well, then thicken it with grated Bread and Oat-meal finely beaten, of each a like quantity; with Beef suet finely shred and Marrow in little lumps. Season it with a little Nutmeg and Cloves and Mace mingled with Salt, Sweet Marjoram, Thyme and Pennyroyal shred very well together: some put in a few Currants. Mingle all this well, and pour it into a skin of cleansed Guts, tied at one end: then tie the other end, and boil the Puddings carefully.'

The Closet of Sir Kenelm Digby Opened 1669

Gather yarrow, still flowering in most years: destroy troublesome ants' nests.

13

'An ointment of yarrow cures wounds, and is most fit for such as have inflammations. It stays the shedding of the hair, the head being bathed with the decoction of it; inwardly taken, it helps the retentive faculty of the stomach . . . and such as cannot hold their water; and the leaves chewed in the mouth ease the tooth-ache.'

Culpeper *Herbal* 1653

'To destroy Ants Nests. Pare the turf off and lay the nest open. Then cut out the core below the surface, so deep that when you lay back the turves, the place may be lower than the other ground, to the end that the water may stand in it to prevent the ant from returning, which otherwise she will assuredly do. The proper season for this is November.'

John Worlidge *Systema Agriculturae* 1697

Be sure to lay in stocks of winter firewood.

14

Beechwood fires burn bright and clear
If the logs be kept a year
Oaken logs if dry and old
Keep away the winter's cold
Chesnut's only good they say
If for years 'tis laid away
But ash-wood green or ash-wood brown
Are fit for a King with a golden crown.

Elm she burns like the churchyard mould
Even the very flames are cold
Birch and pine-wood burn too fast
Blaze too bright and do not last
But ash wet or ash dry
A Queen may warm her slippers by.

On this day in 1635 died Old Parr of Shropshire, who claimed to have been born in 1483 and thus to be 152 years old. He married for the first time at 80, and for the second at 120: but the excitement of a visit to Charles I's court proved fatal to him, and he is buried in Westminster Abbey.

15

Keep up your spirits with healthy exercise: treat throat complaints betimes.

'Leaping is an exercise very commendable and healthful to the body, especially if you use it in the morning: but upon a full stomach and to bedward it is very dangerous, and in no wise to be used.'

Henry Peacham *The Compleat Gentleman* 1634

'Wrestling is a very good exercise in the beginning of youth, so that it be with one that is equal in strength or somewhat under, and that the place be soft, that in falling their bodies be not bruised . . . but in football is nothing but beastly fury and extreme violence, whereof proceedeth hurt, and consequently rancour and malice do remain with them that be wounded. Wherefore it is to be put to perpetual silence.'

Sir Thomas Elyot *The Book Named the Governor* 1531

'How to help one that hath the Squincy in the throat. Take the old nest of a swallow with all the substance (as clay, gravel, sticks and feathers): do nothing but beat it and sift it through a coarse sieve, and put thereto grease and honey and make a plaster thereof. Then stroke it upon a cloth and lay it about his neck: of this wise have I holpen one in three hours.'

John Hollybush *The Homish Apothecary* 1561

16

Cleanse privies, trench gardens, sweep chimneys.

Foul privies are now to be cleansed and fide
Let night be appointed, such baggage to hide
Which buried in gardens, in trenches a-low
Shall make very many things better to grow.

The chimney all sooty would now be made clean
For fear of mischances, too oftentimes seen
Old chimney and sooty, if fire once take
By burning and breaking, soon mischief may make.

Tusser *Five Hundred Points of Good Husbandry* 1573

NOVEMBER

Queen Elizabeth's Holiday: the anniversary of her Accession to the throne in 1558, formerly much celebrated with bonfires and bellringing.

'Next came the Queen, in the sixty-sixth year of her age, as we were told, but very majestic: her face was oblong, fair, but wrinkled; her eyes small, but black and pleasant; her nose a little hooked, her lips narrow, and her teeth black . . . She had in her ears two pearls, with very rich drops; she wore false hair, and that red.'

Paul Hentzner *Travels in England* 1598

'Sometimes she recreated herself in playing upon the Lute and Virginals. She asked me, if she played well? I said, reasonably, for a Queen. . . . She enquired of me, whether she or my Queen danced best. I answered, Queen Mary danced not so high and disposedly as she did.'

Sir James Melville *Memoirs* 1560s

Make sausages from pork offcuts: observe the fingernails.

'To make very fine sausages. Take four pound and a half of pork, chop it small, and put to it three pounds of beef suet, and chop them small together. Then put to them a handful of Sage finely shred, one ounce of pepper, one ounce of mace, two ounces of cloves, a good deal of salt, and eight eggs very well beaten before you put them in. Work them well with your hand till they be thoroughly mingled, and then fill the skins with the mixture.'

Thomas Jenner *A Book of Fruits and Flowers* 1653

'The nails very short, signify a person to be wicked; small and cracked, to be a greedy catcher; very little, to be a crafty beguiler. White flecks in the nails signifies very wealthy, and to have many friends: black flecks, to be hated. The nails long, smooth, reddish and clear withal, to be witty and of a good capacity; narrow and long, to be cruel and fierce; the nails rough and round, to be prone to the venereal act.'

The Shepherd's Prognostication 1729

19

Night-fowling now in season.

'The Air being mild and the Moon not shining, you shall take your Low-Bell, which is a Bell such as a man may carry in one hand, having a deep, hollow and sad sound, the more sad and solemn the better. You shall also have a Net at least twenty yards deep, according as you have company to carry it. With these instruments you shall go into some stubble field, and he which carrieth the Bell shall go the foremost and toll the Bell as he goeth along solemnly. Then having spread your Net where you think any Game is, you shall light bundles of dry Straw that will blaze . . . and with noises and poles beat all up that are under the Net. For the use of these instruments is, that the sound of the Bell makes the birds to lie close whilst you are pitching your Net, for the sound thereof is dreadful to them . . . then the suddenness of the light blazing (which they can far worse endure than the Bell) makes them to spring up, while the Net stays and entangles them.'

Markham *Hunger's Prevention* 1621

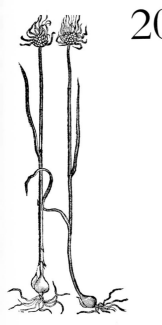

20

The Feast of St Edmund of East Anglia: plant garlic and beans.

St Edmund, the Saxon king of East Anglia, was martyred by invading Vikings on this day in 869. He was first tied to an oak and shot full of arrows and then beheaded, his head being hidden in a thorn bush: but when his followers sought it, the head itself was heard crying 'Here, here', and was discovered in the care of a monstrous white wolf. Enshrined at Bury St Edmunds, the much venerated king became the special patron of sailors, and was for several centuries effectively the patron saint of England.

Set garlic and beans, at St Edmund the King
The moon in the wane, thereof hangeth a thing.

'Garlic sodden down with milk or broken and mingled with soft cheese stauncheth the falling down of humours called cattarh: and so it is good against hoarseness. Three little cloves broken in vinegar and laid to the teeth are good for the teeth ache. . . . Garlic driveth away with his smell serpents and venomous beasts.'

William Turner *Herbal* 1568

Traditionally the day on which Noah entered the Ark: Stir-Up Sunday falls about now.

21

Stir-Up Sunday is the last Sunday before Advent, when the Church of England collect begins: 'Stir up, we beseech thee, O Lord, the wills of thy faithful people . . .' This was taken as a reminder to 'stir up' the mixture for Christmas puddings and pies, in order to allow them plenty of time to mature, and was parodied as

> Stir up, we beseech thee
> The pudding in the pot
> And when we do get home
> We'll eat it piping hot.

Christmas puddings and pies should always be stirred clockwise with a wooden spoon: all present should take a turn in order – mother, father, children and babies by seniority, and visitors.

Martinmas, Old Style: hiring fairs for farm-labourers and servants now held in northern England and Scotland.

22

> Servant men, stand up for your wages
> When to the hirings you do go
> For you must work all sorts of weather
> Both cold and wet and snow.
>
> Ballad, Clun, Shropshire

Also called Pack-Rag Day, because servants now carried their possessions to their new work-places.

Northern labourers now returned home for their annual week's holiday: there gargantuan meals were prepared for them on Old Martinmas Sunday, hence called 'Rive-kite [split-stomach] Sunday' in Yorkshire.

'For one that is sick upon a full stomach. Take fennel and chew it in thy mouth. Spit out some and take down some. It is a present remedy.'
Fairfax Household Book, 17th/18th century

23 St Clement's Day: the blacksmiths' holiday.

St Clement, an early Bishop of Rome, was traditionally martyred by being tied to an iron anchor and drowned in the sea. Hence he is the patron of mariners and iron-workers, especially blacksmiths – who on this day 'fired their anvils' by exploding gunpowder on them and held 'Old Clem' processions.

In the Midlands, children went 'Clementing' for fruit and pennies on this day, singing

St Clements, St Clements comes once in a year
Apples and pears are very good cheer
Got no apples, money will do
Please to give us one of the two
Father's at work and Mother's at play
Please to remember St Clement's Day

Walsall, Staffordshire

24 The Sun enters the House of Sagittarius.

'The man born under Sagittarius shall have mercy on every man he sees. He shall go far to desert places unknown and dangerous, and shall return with great gains: he shall see his fortune increase from day to day. At twenty-two years he shall have some peril, but he shall live seventy-two years and eight months after nature.

'The woman shall love to labour: she may not see one weep without pity. She shall spend much silver by evil company. She ought to be married at thirteen years, and shall have pain in her eyes at fourteen: she shall be called the mother of sons, and shall live seventy-two years after nature.

'Both man and woman shall be inconstant in deeds; but of good conscience, merciful, and better to others than themselves.' *Kalendar of Shepheardes* 1604

St Catherine's Day: the spinsters' and lace-makers' feast.

25

According to legend, St Catherine was a virgin princess who refused to marry a pagan Emperor; and was therefore condemned to be broken on a spiked wheel – whence the familiar 'catherine wheel'. She is therefore the patron of all who use the wheel, especially carters and spinners – as well as unmarried girls, who celebrated her day with hot ale and pies.

> Rise, maidens, rise
> Bake your Cattern pies
> Bake enough and bake no waste
> And let the Bellman have a taste

Because of the confusion with Queen Catherine of Aragon, who is said to have burned all her lace and ordered new when times were hard, St Catherine was also honoured by lace-makers. On her day, these jumped for luck over a lighted candle in a candlestick.

> Kit be nimble, Kit be quick
> Kit jump o'er the candlestick.

'We have a custom, yet in mode, that when one sneezes everyone pulls off his hat, and bows, and cries, "God bless ye, Sir".'

26

John Aubrey *Remains of Gentilism* 1688

'Concerning Sternutation or Sneezing, and the custom of saluting or blessing upon that motion, it is pretended and generally believed to derive its original from a disease wherein Sternutation proved fatal, and such as Sneezed died. . . . Yet Sneezing being properly a motion of the brain, suddenly expelling through the nostrils what is offensive to it, it cannot but afford some evidence of mental vigour.'

Sir Thomas Browne *Pseudodoxia Epidemica* 1646

Sneezing to the left hand is held to be unlucky, but sneezing to the right is prosperous.

'Many will go to bed again, if they but sneeze before their shoes be on their feet: as some will hold fast their left thumb with their right hand when they hiccup, or else will hold their chin with their right hand while a gospel is sung.'

Reginald Scot *Discovery of Witchcraft* 1584

27

Eels now in season for baked eel pies.

'To take Eels in Winter. Make a long bottle or tube of Hay, wrapped about Willow boughs, and having guts or garbage in the middle. Which being soaked in the deep water by the river side, after two or three days the eels will be in it, and you may tread them out with your feet.'

Markham *The English Husbandman* 1635

'To bake Eels in a pie. After you have drawn your eels, chop them into pieces three or four inches long, and put them in a pan: season them with Pepper, Salt, Ginger, great Raisins and Onions small chopped, and cover them with Stock. Then boil them gently until the flesh will easily come from the bones. Put the flesh into a pie dish with a small piece of lemon, a good lump of butter, and enough of your stock to cover them: then put on your cover of pastry and bake your pie very hot, about three quarters of an hour.'

Mistress King's Receipt Book, mid 17th century

28

Last chance for weddings before Advent, during which season they were frowned upon: be careful to choose an auspicious colour for the wedding dress.

> Marry in green, ashamed to be seen
> Marry in grey, you'll go far away
> Marry in brown, never live in a town
> Marry in red, wish yourself dead
> Marry in yellow, ashamed of your fellow
> Marry in black, wish yourself back
> Marry in pink, of you he'll aye think
> Marry in blue, love ever true
> Marry in white, you have chosen right.

'When a man designs to marry a woman who is in debt, if he takes her from the hands of the priest clothed only in her shift, it is supposed that he will not then be liable for her obligations.'

The Gentleman's Magazine 1784

29

Snow not unusual at this time, especially on high ground.

'If great black Clouds come out of the North, and appear whitish when nearer to you, and the season be cold and dry, it signifies Snow or Hail; if the fire burns violently and makes a noise like one treading of Snow, that presageth usually Snow; if the hair of dogs smells stronger than usual, or if their guts rumble and make a noise, or if they tumble up and down, that foreshows Snow or Rain.'

John Worlidge *Systema Agriculturae* 1696

'To make a Snow-tree by artifice. Take a quart of thick Cream and five or six whites of Eggs, a saucer full of Sugar and as much Rose-water: beat them all together and as your froth riseth always take it out with a spoon. Then take a loaf of Bread, cut away the crust, set it in a platter, and set a Rosemary bush in the midst of your loaf. Then lay your Snow-froth upon the Rosemary, and so serve it.'

Thomas Jenner *A Book of Fruits and Flowers* 1653

30

St Andrew the King
Three weeks and three days before Christmas comes in.

St Andrew, the first-called of the Apostles, was in fact a Galilean fisherman, the brother of St Peter: who according to legend was martyred on an X-shaped 'St Andrew's Cross'. He is the patron of fishers and fishmongers, of Russia and Scotland: his relics are said to have been brought to St Andrews in Fife during the fourth century.

In Scotland, the traditional dishes on this day are boiled or baked sheep's head, haggis and whisky.

In parts of Kent and Sussex, the right to hunt squirrels at St Andrewstide was claimed: 'when the lower kind of people assembling together form a lawless rabble, and being accoutred with guns, poles, clubs and other such weapons, spend the greatest part of the day in parading through the woods . . . and under pretence of demolishing the squirrels (some few of which they kill) they destroy numbers of hares, pheasants and partridges and, in short, whatever comes in their way.'

Hasted *History of Kent* 1782

DECEMBER

THE MONTH OF CHRISTMAS

The tenth month of the Roman calendar.
In Welsh: *Rhagfyr* – the month of preparation.
In Gaelic: *An Mios marbh* – the dead month
In Anglo-Saxon: *Giuli* – the month of Yule.

DECEMBER

O Dirty December
Yet Christmas remember.

1

'This month keep thy body and head from cold: let thy Kitchen be thine Apothecary, warm clothing thy Nurse, merry company thy Keepers, and good hospitality thine Exercise.'

Neve's *Almanack* 1633

'On December the First 1750, for a wager, seven men were buttoned without straining into the waistcoat of Mr Edward Bright of Maldon, Essex; who lately deceased at the age of twenty-nine, and who was esteemed to be the fattest man that ever lived in Britain. He weighed about fifty-one and a half stone, and stood above five feet nine inches tall: his frame was of an astonishing bulk, and his legs were as thick as a middling man's body, yet he was surprisingly active.'

Hone *Every-Day Book* 1829

The season of Advent, the time of preparation for Christ's 'coming' (in Latin *adventus*) begins about now – on Advent Sunday, which is the fourth before Christmas: children kept indoors by bad weather.

2

'There is no better use of having your children noisy and troublesome, than this of plaguing all your acquaintance. For you may suffer them, when you have visitors, to make such a racket that you cannot hear one another speak. Let them also, with their greasy fingers, soil and besmear your visitors' clothes; put their fingers and dirty noses (if you are drinking tea) into the cream pot, and dribble over the sugar; throw the remainder of the cream over somebody's clean gown; and thrust bread and butter down the ladies' backs: and in short, be more troublesome and offensive than squirrels, parrots or monkeys.'

Jane Collier *The Art of Ingeniously Tormenting* 1753

3

Hutch-rabbits, or 'rich Conies', now in prime condition.

'All sorts of Conies may as well be kept tame as wild, and . . . their delight is to live in holes and dark caverns. Yet they are violently hot in the act of generation, and perform it with such vigour and excess, that they swound and lie in trances a good space after. . . . Every one of your rich Conies which are killed in season (as from Martinmas until after Candlemas) is worth any five other Conies, for they are of body much fatter and larger, and their skins incomparably better than the wild sort.'

Markham *Cheap and Good Husbandry* 1683

'To gild a spit-roasted Coney. Mix one gill of cream with a little flour, parsley chopped small, two egg yolks, pepper, salt and nutmeg grated; when the coney is almost roasted, paint it all over with this paste; and when the paste is dried on, baste it with fresh butter until it is done. This makes a rich gravy, and puts away the Coney's dryness.'

Lyon's Receipt Book, 1690

4

St Barbara's Day: the gunner's holiday.

The legendary St Barbara was imprisoned in a high tower by her father to discourage her many suitors. But Christian books were smuggled in to her, and when her father learned of her conversion he handed her over for torture and eventually beheaded her himself – whereupon he was instantly struck dead by lightning. She is thus invoked against tempests and explosions, and is the particular patron of artillerymen.

'A very good receipt for one hurt with Gunpowder. Take twelve heads of houseleek, a handful of groundsel, one pint of goose-dung, and as much chicken-dung of the newest that can be gotten. Stamp the herbs very small, then put the dung into the mortar, temper it with boar's grease, and stir all together half an hour. Strain it through a canvas bag, and so preserve it for your use: it will keep two years and be not the worse.'

Hannah Woolley *The Gentlewoman's Companion* 1675

December

The best time to rid gardens of snails: inspect cider stocks against Christmas.

'The best way to take Snails, is to set Tiles, Bricks or Boards hollow against a wall or otherwise: so that the Snails may seek shelter under them. Then about Michaelmas the Snails secure themselves in such places for the whole Winter, unless you prevent them by taking them in early December and destroying them, which is an easy and safe way to rid your garden of them.'

Worlidge *Systema Agriculturae* 1697

'Half a peck of unground Wheat put to Cider that is harsh and eager will renew its fermentation, and render it more mild and gentle. A little quantity of Mustard will clear an hogshead of muddy Cider: and the same Virtue is ascribed to two or three rotten apples put into it.'

John Newburgh *Observations on Cider* 1678

The Feast of St Nicholas: Boy Bishops appointed.

St Nicholas was a fourth-century bishop of Myra in Asia Minor, who was so pious even as a baby that he would only suckle once on fast days. He is said to have saved three maidens from prostitution by covertly throwing three golden balls for their dowries through their window by night: and to have miraculously revived three murdered boys pickled in a brine-tub. He is thus the special patron of children (as well as of pawnbrokers, who use his three golden balls as a sign) and his nocturnal kindness is perpetuated in the gifts left by 'Sinte Klaas' – the Dutch-American version of his name.

'In Sarum Cathedral is a little monument of a Boy Bishop, who died in his office. . . . The Tradition is, that this Child-Bishop being melancholy, the Children of the Choir did tickle him to make him merry; but they did so over-do it, that they tickled him to death.'

John Aubrey *Remains of Gentilism* 1688

7

Protect plants against frost, especially rosemary for Christmas decorations.

Evergreen rosemary – the rose of the Virgin Mary – is one of the special plants of Christmas. It was believed to blossom at midnight on Christmas Eve, and to have acquired its scent from the garments of the Infant Jesus, which the Virgin hung out to dry on a rosemary bush.

'Rosemary comforteth the brain, the memory, and the inward senses. The distilled water of the flowers, being drunk morning and evening, taketh away the stench of the mouth and breath, and maketh it very sweet.'

Gerard's *Herbal* 1636

'A sprig of rosemary boiled for a quarter of an hour in cider, and the cider drunk very hot to bedward, will cure a cold by much sweating.'

John Lloyd's Book, 1720

'Where rosemary grows, the woman rules the house.'

8

Observe the day of the week on which babies are born.

'Who that is born on a Sunday shall be great and shining; he that is born on the Monday shall prosper, if he begin any work on that day. Who that is born on Tuesday shall be covetous, and perish by iron, and hardly come to his last age: he that is born on Wednesday shall lightly learn words; on Thursday they that are born shall be stable and worshipful. He that is born on Friday shall be of long life and very lecherous: but who that is born on Saturday shall seldom be profitable, but if the course of the Moon bring it about.'

The Knowledge of Things Unknown 1729

Monday's child is fair of face
Tuesday's child is full of grace
Wednesday's child is full of woe
Thursday's child has far to go
Friday's child is loving and giving
Saturday's child works hard for a living
But the child that's born on the Sabbath day
Is bonny and blithe and good and gay.

DECEMBER

Robins now much in evidence, singing their winter song.

9

Robins have long been associated with Christmas charity, perhaps because their red breasts were believed to be stained by Christ's blood, which spurted there when a kindly robin tried to pluck a prickle from the Crown of Thorns.

>   Covering with moss the dead's unclosed eye
>   The little red-breast teacheth charity.

Robins were also said to charitably cover the unburied corpses of the murdered with moss and leaves, as they did for the legendary 'Babes in the Wood'.

>   No Burial this pretty pair
>   Of any man receives
>   Till Robin Redbreast painfully
>   Did cover them with leaves.
>   Percy's *Reliques* 1765

It is very unlucky to kill or cage a robin or a wren, or to take their eggs, since

>   The Robin Redbreast and the Wren
>   Are God Almighty's Cock and Hen.

Lay in stocks of Christmas firewood: make jumble-biscuits.

10

>   No season to hedge
>   Get beetle and wedge
>   Cleave logs now all
>   For kitchen and hall.
>   Tusser *Five Hundred Points of Good Husbandry* 1573

'To make Knots or Jumballs. Take twelve yolks of eggs and five whites; a pound of sugar, half a pound of butter washed in rose water, three-quarters of an ounce of mace finely beaten, a little salt dissolved in rose water, half an ounce of aniseeds and half an ounce of caraway seeds. Mingle all these together with as much flour as will work it up into paste, and so mould it into knots or rings of what fashion you please. Then bake your jumbals hard upon pie-plates, and so serve them forth when you serve hot spiced wine.'
>   Fairfax Household Book, 17th/18th century

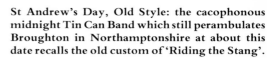

11

St Andrew's Day, Old Style: the cacophonous midnight Tin Can Band which still perambulates Broughton in Northamptonshire at about this date recalls the old custom of 'Riding the Stang'.

'Riding the Stang', or the 'Skimmington Ride', was a very public display of disapproval, directed at wife-beaters, husband-beaters, adulterers or other like offenders. The erring man or woman themselves (if they could be caught) or someone representing them, or else a straw dummy, was paraded through the streets astride a 'stang' or pole: and behind this marched the Ran-Tan Band, beating pans and kettles, blowing horns, and singing insulting songs. Outside the offender's house a speech recounting their 'crime' was made, and sometimes the straw effigy was burnt. This ceremony was repeated on three nights in succession, and if the offenders had any sense they did not stay long in the village afterwards.

12

St Finnian's Night in the Scottish Highlands and Islands: it is very unlucky to go to bed supperless on this night, and anyone who did so was likely to be carried over the housetop by the fairies.

'Francis Fry returning from Work was caught by the Woman Spectre by the Skirts of his Doublet, and carried into the Air . . . and about half an Hour after he was heard Whistling and Singing in a Kind of a Quagmire. Coming to himself an Hour after, he solemnly protested, that the Daemon carried him so high he saw his Master's House underneath him no bigger than an Hay-cock . . . he prayed God not to suffer the Devil to destroy him; and he was then suddenly set down in that Quagmire. The workmen found one Shoe on one side of the House, and the other shoe on the other side; his Perriwig was espied next Morning hanging on top of a Tall Tree.'
Letter to Aubrey from the minister of Barnstaple,
Devon, 1683

December

St Lucy's Day: seek cures for sore eyes.

13

St Lucy or Lucia was a fourth-century virgin martyr of Syracuse in Sicily. Because her name means 'light', she is an appropriate patron for this day, one of the darkest and shortest in the year according to the old calendar: and for the same reason she is invoked against eye diseases.

'For the redness of the eyes, or bloodshot. Take red wine, red rose water and woman's milk, and mingle all these together: and cut a piece of wheaten bread leavened, as much as will cover the eye, and lay it in the mixture. When you go to bed, lay the bread upon your eyes, and it will help them.'
                    Fairfax Household Book, 17th/18th century

'Things hurtful to the eyes: Garlic, Onions, Radish, Drunkenness, Lechery, Sweet Wines, salt Meats, Coleworts, Dust, Smoke, and Reading presently after Supper. Good for the eyes: Fennel, Celandine, Eyebright, Vervain, Roses, Cloves and cold Water.'
                    White's *Almanack* 1627

Mark where mistletoe grows, for Christmas decorations: but on no account bring it into the house until Christmas Eve.

14

Most powerful of all against evil is the rare oak-mistletoe, which should be gathered at New Moon without the use of iron, and never allowed to touch the ground: but mistletoe grown on apple trees or the sacred hawthorn is also especially worth having.

'Some women have worn mistletoe about their necks or arms, thinking it will help them to conceive.'
                    William Coles *Adam in Eden* 1657

Mistletoe is likewise an aphrodisiac and a plant of fertility, hence perhaps the originally Welsh Border custom of kissing beneath mistletoe boughs decked with ribbons, nuts and apples. After each kiss, the lady concerned should pluck a berry and throw it over her left shoulder; and when the berries come to an end, so should the kissing.

15

Even in cold weather, beware of taking cats to bed for warmth.

'As this beast the Cat hath been familiarly nourished of many, so have they paid dear for their love, being requited with the loss of their health and sometimes of their life. . . . For it is most certain, that the breath and savour of Cats consume the radical humour and destroy the lungs, and therefore they which keep their Cats with them in their beds have the Air corrupted, and fall into several Hecticks and Consumptions.'

Edward Topsell *History of Four-footed Beasts* 1607

16

Called 'O Sapientia' ('O Wisdom') by the Church, from the anthem sung today: traditionally the beginning of the mince pie season.

'The best receipt for Minced Pie mixture. One pound of tripe well shred or thirteen eggs hard-boiled with half the whites taken out; two pounds of suet well shred as small as possible; one pound raisins; two pounds of prunes stoned and shred; one pound currants and half an ounce of nuts; cinnamon, mace and cloves a quarter ounce each; eight sour apples shred; one gill each of verjuice, sack and brandy; and half a pound of lemon peel with sugar.'

Fairfax Household Book, 17th/18th century

Originally rectangular in shape, and said to represent Christ's manger, mince pies were abominated as 'Popish and superstitious' by Puritans, and described thus in 1656:

Idolatry in crust! Babylon's whore
Defiled with superstition, like the Gentiles
Of Old, that worshipped onions, roots, and lentils.

Later, however, the 'solid, substantial, Protestant mince pie' became the champion of the English Christmas against 'imported foreign kickshaws'.

Eat mince pies made by as many different cooks as possible: for every cook's pie, you will have a lucky month in the coming year.

Feed bees, especially in hard weather or after a poor summer.

17

> Go look to thy bees, if the hive be too light
> Set honey and water, with rosemary dight
> Which set in a dish full of sticks in the hive
> From danger of famine will save them alive.
> Tusser *Five Hundred Points of Good Husbandry* 1573

> Bees, bees, awake
> Your master is dead
> And another you must take.

Bees must be formally 'told' when the head of the household dies — or indeed of any other important news — lest they fly away to seek the departed, or die themselves: and in Devonshire it was believed that all hives must be turned or moved at the moment their dead owner's corpse left the house for burial.

Look for Christmas holly and ivy: but do not put them up until Christmas Eve.

18

The most universally popular of Christmas ever-greens, holly's red berries symbolize Christ's blood, and its prickles his Crown of Thorns: and even before the coming of Christianity it was valued as a sure preservative against both lightning and witchcraft — whence the holly trees planted outside northern farmhouse doors.

Ivy, whose black berries do not ripen until Christmas-time, after the hard frosts, has many medicinal as well as magical uses, and is 'a plant of Bacchus': 'The berries taken before one be set to drink hard, preserve from drunkenness . . . and if one hath got a surfeit by drinking of wine, the speediest cure is to drink a draught of the same wine wherein a handful of ivy leaves (being first bruised) have been boiled.'
Culpeper *Herbal* 1653

19

Prepare to look your best for Christmas: but beware indiscretions.

'To make the skin of the hands and face very smooth. Take Almonds and beat them to an oil, then take whole Cloves and put them together in a glass: and set this in the sun five or six days. Then strain it, and with the same anoint yourself every night when you go to bed.'

Mistress Whitnall's Book, 18th century

'Gentlewomen, I am not insensible that you frequent places of eminency for resort, which cannot but offer to your view a variety of Pleasing Objects. Nay, there where nothing but chaste thoughts, staid looks and modest desires should harbour, are too commonly loose thoughts, light looks and licentious desires. The means to prevent this Malady, is to abate your esteem for any earthly Object. Do you admire the Comeliness of any creature? Remove your eye from thence, and bestow it on the super-excellency of your Creator.'

Hannah Woolley *The Gentlewoman's Companion* 1675

20

St Thomas's Eve: divine the future, but beware of ghosts.

Stick a pin in the exact centre of an onion and range eight more pins round the first in a circle, repeating

> Good St Thomas, do me right
> And let my true love come to-night
> That I may see him in the face
> And in my arms may him embrace.

Then put the onion under your pillow, and you will dream of your future husband.

By tradition, ghosts are permitted to walk abroad from now until Christmas Eve:

'They have so frayed us with bull-beggers, spirits, witches, urchins, hags, elves, fairies, satyrs, pans, fauns, sylens, kit-with-the-canstick, centaurs, dwarfs, giants, imps, calcars, conjurors, nymphs, changelings, Incubus, Robin Good-fellow, the spoorn, the mare, the man in the Oak, the hell-wain, the firedrake, the puckle, Tom Thumb, Hob Goblin, Tom Tumbler, Boneless and other such Bugs, that we are afraid of our own shadows.'

Reginald Scot *The Discovery of Witchcraft* 1584

December

St Thomas grey, St Thomas grey
The longest night and the shortest day.

21

The Winter Solstice, and the Feast of St Thomas the Apostle, called 'doubting Thomas' because he questioned the Resurrection. He is the patron of carpenters and masons.

> St Thomas goes too soon away
> Then your gooding we do pray
> Please to remember St Thomas's Day.

All over England, poorer women and children went 'Thomassing' today for Christmas 'goodenings', especially wheat for frumenty and flour for Yule Bread.

On this day the Sheriffs of York proclaimed the Christmas amnesty for petty criminals, in these words: 'We command that the peace of our Lord the King be well kept by night and day. . . . But that all manner of whores, thieves, dice-players and other unthrifty folk be welcome to the city, whether they come late or early, at the reverence of the high feast of Yule, till the twelve days be passed.'

The Sun enters the House of Capricorn.

22

'The man born under Capricorn shall be iracundious and a fornicator: a liar, and always labouring. He shall be a governor of beasts with four feet. He shall suffer much sorrow in his youth, but shall leave many goods and riches. He shall have great peril at sixteen years. He shall be rich by women, and shall be a great conductor of maidens: he shall live seventy years and four months after nature.

'The woman shall be honest and fearful, and have children of three men: she will do many pilgrimages in her youth, and after have great wit. She shall have great goods, but pain in her eyes, and shall be at her best estate at thirty years: she shall live seventy years after nature.'

Kalendar of Shepheardes 1604

23 Observe the day on which Christmas falls, and the weather.

'If Christmas Day fall on a Sunday, that year shall be a warm Winter, the Summer hot and dry: peace and quietness shall be plenteous among married folks. If on a Monday, a misty Winter, the Summer windy and stormy: and many women mourning their husbands. On Tuesday, a cold Winter and much snow, the Summer wet: but good peace shall be among Kings and Princes. On Wednesday, the Winter naughty and hard, the Summer very good: young people and cattle shall die sore. On Thursday, the Winter mild and Summer very good and abundant: many great men shall perish. On Friday, the Winter neither bad nor good, and the Harvest indifferent. . . . On Saturday, the Winter with great wind, snow and cold, the Summer good: there shall be war in many lands.'

The Knowledge of Things Unknown 1729

'Resolved by the Parliament, December the Twenty-third 1652. That no Observation shall be had of the five-and-twentieth day of December, commonly called Christ-mass Day.'

Parliamentary Journal 1652

The Vindication of
CHRISTMAS

Keep out, you come not here,

O Sir, I bring good chere.

Old Christmas welcome; Do not fear...

24 Christmas Eve: put up decorations, light the Christmas Candle, and bring in the Yule Log.

Come bring with a noise; My merry, merry boys
The Christmas log to the firing
With the last year's brand; Light the new block, and
    For good success in his spending
On your psaltries play; That sweet luck may
    Come while the log is a-teending.

Herrick *Hesperides* 1648

The Yule Log or Christmas Brand must never be bought, but should be given, 'found', or taken from your own property. It should not be brought in until today, and should be lit at dusk, using a fragment of last year's log: it should then burn at least all night – or if possible throughout the coming Twelve Days of Christmas – without going out, though it may be extinguished. The piece kept to light next year's log will protect the house from fire.

The Christmas candle should preferably be red, and should be big enough to light the evening meal on each of the next Twelve Days. It must never blow out accidentally.

December

Christmas Day: the Birth-day (in Latin 'dies natalis') of Our Lord – *Nadolig* in Welsh and *Nollaig* in Gaelic.

25

At Christmas be merry and thankful withall
  And feast thy poor neighbours, the great with the
                                                small
Yea, all the year long, to the poor let us give
  God's blessing to follow us while we do live.
  Tusser *Five Hundred Points of Good Husbandry* 1573

Some say, that ever 'gainst that season comes
Wherein our Saviour's birth is celebrated
The bird of dawning singeth all night long
And, then, they say, no sprite can walk abroad
The nights are wholesome; then no Planets strike
No fairy takes, nor witch hath power to charm
So hallowed and so gracious is the time.
              Shakespeare *Hamlet* Act I, Scene I, 1601

Merry Christmas; *Nadolig Llawen*; *Nollaig faoi shean*;
                                          God Jul.

Boxing Day: St Stephen's Day: the First Day of Christmas.

26

  When Boxing Day comes round again
  O then I shall have money
  I'll hoard it up, and Box and all
  I'll give it to my honey.

On this day tradesmen, servants and children went 'Boxing', soliciting Christmas tips from householders they had served during the year. These were put into slitted earthenware 'Christmas Boxes'.

The Feast of St Stephen, whose proximity to Christmas reflects his status as the first Christian martyr.

  The Wren, the Wren, the King of All Birds
  St Stephen's Day was caught in the furze
  Although he be little, his honour is great
  Therefore good people, give us a treat.

On this day alone, the usually sacred and protected wren was ceremonially hunted, and its decorated corpse carried about by luck-bringing 'Wren Boys'.

27

St John's Day: the Second Day of Christmas: observe the weather, and be careful how much Christmas chocolate you eat.

St John, apostle and Gospel-maker, was traditionally 'the disciple whom Jesus loved' (*John* XIII 23). He is the patron of booksellers, publishers, printers and writers.

'What weather shall be on the sixth and twentieth day of December, the like weather shall be all the month of January: what shall be on the seventh and twentieth, the like shall be the following February, and so on until Twelfth Day: each day's weather foreshowing a month of the year.'

Gervase Markham *The English Husbandman* 1635

'The Confection made of Cacao called Chocolate or Chocoletto, which may be had in divers places in London at reasonable rates, is of wonderful efficacy for the procreation of children: for it not only vehemently incites to Venus, but causeth Conception in women . . . and besides that it preserves health, for it makes such as take it often to become fat and corpulent, fair and amiable.'

William Coles *Adam in Eden* 1657

28

Holy Innocents' Day or Childermass: the Third Day of Christmas, and the unluckiest day of the year.

The Holy Innocents were the Bethlehem 'childer' of two years old and under, who were slaughtered by Herod in an attempt to eliminate the Infant Jesus. Special kindness should be shown to children today, and in some places they were even allowed to play in churches. Because of its dismal associations, this day is exceedingly ill-omened for working, for beginning any new enterprise whatever, or even for wearing new clothes. Indeed, the day of the week on which it happens to fall will be unfortunate throughout the year.

To play the old Christmas game of Snap-Dragon, pour brandy over a bowl of raisins and set fire to it. Then turn out the lights, and let each person in turn try to snatch a raisin from the flames.

> Here he comes with flaming bowl
> Don't he mean to take his toll
>   Snip! Snap! Dragon!
> Don't 'ee fear him, but be bold
> Out he goes, his flames are cold
>   Snip! Snap! Dragon.

DECEMBER

St Thomas of Canterbury's Day: the Fourth Day of Christmas: wassailing in full swing.

Wassailing – whose name derives from the Anglo-Saxon toast *Waes Heil*, meaning 'Good Health' – is the custom of drinking communally from a large bowl. Such bowls were carried from house to house by carol-singers, who expected the householders to fill them with hot spiced 'lamb's wool'.

> Wassail, wassail, all over the town
> Our bread it is white and our ale it is brown
> Our bowl it is made from good maple tree
> We be good fellows all; I drink unto thee.
> The Gloucestershire Wassail

'To make Lamb's Wool. To every quart of good ale put a pint of white wine, and heat them well together. Then put in cinnamon and nutmeg grated and sugar, with roasted crab apples and if you will some toasts to float thereon, and serve it forth in a bowl very hot.'
Mistress Watkinson's Book, mid 17th century

The Fifth Day of Christmas: perform Christmas Mumming Plays, and seek cures for excessive wassailing.

In comes I, Old Father Christmas; welcome or welcome not
I hope Old Father Christmas; will never be forgot
If you don't believe what I do say
Enter St George and clear the way

In come I, St George; a man of courage bold
With sword and spear all by my side; hoping to gain a crown of gold
'Twas I that slew the dragon; and brought him to the slaughter
And by those means I hope; to gain the King of Egypt's daughter.
Worcestershire Mummers' Play

'A wonderful experience to cure the headache. Set a dish or platter of tin upon the bare head filled with water, and then drop an ounce and a half or two ounces of molten lead therein while he hath it on his head. That helpeth wonderfully.'
John Hollybush *The Homish Apothecary* 1561

31

New Year's Eve or Hogmanay: the Sixth Day of Christmas.

Be sure to finish today any work you have in hand, for a task carried over into the New Year will never prosper.

Open a bible at random as midnight strikes, and the verse your eye falls on will foretell your luck in the coming year.

> If New Year's Eve night-wind blow south
> That betokens warmth and growth
> If west, much milk, and fish in the sea
> If north, much cold and storms will be
> If east, the trees will bear much fruit
> If north-east, flee it, man and brute.
>
> Scots rhyme

At midnight, prepare to welcome the first visitor of the New Year, whose nature will determine your household's fortune therein. This first-footer (or 'Lucky Bird') should be a tall, well-made man – women first-footers are most unlucky – and in most parts of the country very dark men are preferred and red-heads shunned. He should not be a doctor, minister, lawyer or policeman; he must not wear any black or carry a knife or edged tool; and above all he must come bearing gifts – which should include a loaf, a bottle of whisky, a piece of coal or firing, and perhaps a silver coin. He must enter in silence, and none should speak to him until he has put the coal on the fire, poured a glass for the head of the household, and wished the company

A HAPPY NEW YEAR.

PICTURE CREDITS

Arabic numerals refer to the days of the month, Roman numerals refer to the months.

Frontispiece by Anthony Barton.

Albertina, Vienna 26/III; Ashmolean Museum, Oxford 21/X; T. Bewick 8/I, 18/I, 18/III, 20/III, 29/III, 11/IV, 29/IV, 7/VI, 8/VII, 19/VII, 6/VIII, 4/X, 9/X, 10/XI, 22/XI, 29/XI, 17/XII; Biblioteca Civica, Bergamo 27/II; W. Blake 22/X; Bodleian Library, Oxford 5/V, 25/IX; A. Bosse 26/I, 12/IV, 1/IX, 27/IX, 1/XI, 26/XI, 2/XII, 16/XII; Boymans-van Beuningen Museum, Rotterdam 26/IV; British Library, London 10/III, 6/VI, 18/X; British Museum, London 12/XII, December frontispiece; In the Collection of The Duke of Buccleuch and Queensberry, K.T., at Boughton House, Kettering, England 2/IV; Cheltenham Museum of Art July frontispiece; G. Cruikshank 9/II, 21/II, 22/III, 1/XII; By permission of Viscount De L'Isle, VC, KG, from his collection at Penshurst Place, Kent, England 17/XI; Fundación Lázaro-Galdiano, Madrid 6/XII; J. Gillray 14/V; W. Hogarth 2/I, 17/II, 19/III, 18/V, 5/VIII, 29/VIII, 8/XII, 11/XII, 29/XII; Huntington Library, San Marino, California March frontispiece; Kunsthistorisches Museum, Vienna 17/VI; Louvre, Paris 28/VII; Manchester Free Reference Library 7/IX; Reproduced by permission of the Master and Fellows, Magdalene College, Cambridge 8/V, 19/XII; Mansell Collection 17/I, 29/V; Musée des Augustins, Toulouse 26/VII; Museum of London 4/VII; National Gallery, London 11/VIII; National Portrait Gallery, London 14/XI; Rijksmuseum, Amsterdam 13/I; Royal Museum of Fine Arts, Copenhagen 20/VI; Stadelsches Kunstinstitut, Frankfurt 28/VI; Tate Gallery, London 22/I, 1/II, 12/VII, 28/XI; Victoria and Albert Museum, London 7/X, 29/X

Books

J. Ashton *Chap-Books of the Eighteenth Century* (1882) 23/IV

J. B. Basedow *Elementarwerk* (1774) 21/XII

Bateman's Tragedy; History of Unfortunate Love (1720) front cover, 14/II

S. Bateman *A Cristall Glasse of Christian Reformation* (1569) 29/II

A. Behn *The Ten Pleasures of Marriage* (1682) 3/II, 3/V, 20/V, 20/VII, 25/VIII

E. J. Bennett *The Tower Menagerie* (1829) 1/IV

R. Blome *The Gentleman's Recreation* (1686) 28/I, 11/III, 3/IV, 10/V, 17/IX

Book of Common Prayer (1695) 6/I, 6/II, 27/III, 17/IV, 29/IX, 30/XI, 25/XII

R. Bradley *Gentleman and Farmer's Guide* (1729) 9/XI

Braun and Hogenberg *Civitates Orbis Terrarum* (1572–1618) 7/I

R. Burton *Anatomy of Melancholy* (1628) 25/II

Compleat Astrologer (1587) 28/III

T. Coryat *Crudities* (1611) 5/VII

T. H. Croker *The Complete Dictionary of Arts and Sciences* (1764–66) 13/IX

N. Crouch *Admirable Curiosities* (1682) 22/VIII

—— *The General History of Earthquakes* (1694) 17/X

—— *The Kingdom of Darkness* (1688) 31/X

T. Dekker *A Rod for Runaways* (1625) 16/VIII

J. Dennys *The Secrets of Angling* (1652) 13/IV

Dies Dominica (1639) 20/VIII

E. Digby *De Arte Natandi* (1587) 3/VI

J. Dorat *Magnificentissimj Spectaculi* (1573) 1/VIII

J. Evelyn *The French Gardiner* (1669) 18/VII

F. P. Florin *Oeconomus prudens et leglis* (1705) 15/V

J. Gerard *The Herball* (1636) 14/III, 5/IV, 31/V, 9/VI, 19/VI, 11/VII, 29/VII, 2/VIII, 27/VIII, 30/VIII, 20/XI, 18/XII

J. Glanville *Saducismus Triumphatus* (1700) 30/X, 12/XII

R. Greene *A Quip for an Upstart Courtier* (1592) 18/VI

F. Grose *Antiquities of England and Wales* (1773–87) 14/XII

W. H. von Hohberg *Georgia Curiosa* (1682) 31/I, September frontispiece

W. Hone *Everyday Book* (1826) 20/IV, 23/VI

M. Hopkins *Discoverie of Witches* (1647) 7/XI

J. Janssoon *Hortus floridus* (1614) 17/VIII

R. Johnson *Nova Britannia* (1609) 2/VI

A. Kircher *Arca Noë* (1675) 24/II

C. Knight *The Popular History of England* (1856) 7/II

J. Léger *Histoire générale des églises évangeliques des vallées de Piemont ou vandoises* (1669) 25/VII

D. Loggan *Cantabrigia Illustrata* (1690) 6/IX

E. Marmion *The Genteel Habits of England* (c.1640) 19/XII

Maynus de Mayneriis *Destructorium vitiorum* (1509) 15/IX

Didymus Mountaine (T. Hyll) *The Gardeners' Labyrinth* (1586) 23/I, 15/II, 8/III

Newsletter from the King's Camp at Corbais (July 1696) 24/III

N. de Nicolay *Navigation et Peregrinations* (1568) 28/XII

J. Ogilby *Aesopics, or a Second Collection of Fables Paraphras'd in Verse* (1668) 22/VI

J. Parkinson *Paradisi in Sole, Paradisus Terrestris* (1629) 6/V

Penny Histories (1730) 19/X

J. Perrissin and J. Tortovel *Evénements remarquables* (1559–70) 24/VIII

Petrarch *Trostspiegel* (1596) 13/III

N. Petter *L'Académie de l'Admirable Art de la lutte* (1674) 15/XI

J. Playford *The English Dancing Master* (1651) 9/III

R. Scot *Perfite Platforme of a Hoppe Garden* (1574) 11/IX

Simeonowicz *The Great Art of Artillery* (1694) 4/XII

E. Spenser *The Shepherd's Calendar* (1611) 19/IV, June frontispiece

J. Swammerdam *De Respiratione* (1667) 21/IX

The Tale of Adam Bell, Clim of the Clough and William of Cloudesley (1680s) 8/V

E. Topsell *History of Four-footed Beasts* (1607) 11/II, 15/III, 30/III, 7/IV

J. Vicars *Sight of the Transactions of these Latter Years* (1646) 1/I

G. Walker *The Costume of Yorkshire* (1814) 10/I, 6/X

H. Walpole *Essay on modern gardening* (1785) 10/VI

I. Walton *The Complete Angler* (1878 edn) 25/IV, 27/XI

J. Wilkins *The Discovery of a World in the Moone* (1638) 9/VIII

G. Wither *Emblemes* (1635) 2/III, 3/III, April frontispiece, 10/IV, 14/VI, 3/VII, 28/VIII, 2/X, 6/XI, 5/XII

H. Woolley, *The Accomplisht Lady's Delight* (1677) 26/VI, 7/VII

J. Worlidge *Vinetum Britannicum* (1678) 12/X, 27/X